"Ongoing conflict can sap your energy, destroy relationships, and cost you a job or a marriage. This book provides powerful insights and tools—*beyond* the typical 'use I statements' and 'avoid yes, but' phrasing. Plus, it's a lot less expensive than sitting in a therapist's office!"

—Dianna Booher,
author of fifty books, including *Communicate With Confidence* and *Communicate Like a Leader*

"With four generations currently trying to effectively deal with each other, conflict frequently arises. *A Deeper Connection* presents clear communication tools to resolve the issues. An important read!"

—Dr. Allan Colman,
Author, Speaker, and Revenue Generator

"Most people avoid conflict. Few *thrive* on it. This book offers the tools to build the confidence you need during any conflict. Use these tools and keep the relationship intact even after conflict occurs."

—Janelle Bruland,
Bestselling Author of *The Success Lie*,
9x Inc. Fastest Growing Company

"Connection and conflict show up even in healthy relationships. This book will help you strengthen relationships and resolve conflict quicker."

—Scott Hogle,
President of iHeartMedia
and bestselling author of *Persuade*

A DEEPER CONNECTION

HOW TO NAVIGATE CONFLICT AND GROW RELATIONSHIPS

JOHN SHERRODD

© 2023 John Sherrodd
Published by Made for Success

Made for Success Publishing
P.O. Box 1775 Issaquah, WA 98027
www.MadeForSuccess.com

Distributed by Blackstone Publishing

First Printing

Library of Congress Cataloging-in-Publication data

Sherrodd, John
    A Deeper Connection: How to Navigate Conflict and Grow
    Relationships

        p. cm.

LCCN: 2023943077
ISBN: 978-1-64146-761-2 *(PBBK)*
ISBN: 978-1-64146-771-1 *(eBook)*
ISBN: 978-1-64146-772-8 *(AUDIO)*

Printed in the United States of America

For further information contact Made for Success Publishing
+1425-526-6480 or email service@madeforsuccess.net

This book is dedicated to my amazing wife, Kari Sherrodd—who has always believed in me and my potential, years before I could see it. My love for you continues to grow daily.

I would also like to thank the Emotionally Focused Therapy Community and Sue Johnson for the amazing work they do to help people develop secure attachment and experience more fulfilled lives and relationships. EFT has been transformative in my personal life and my entire approach in my work as a counselor and coach. I cannot thank you enough.

Finally, I want to thank and recognize my clients who have been so brave to vulnerably explore their inner worlds with me. It has been an honor to be trusted and allowed into your thoughts and feelings.

TABLE OF CONTENTS

INTRODUCTION

DO YOU WANT to be happy in life? Have you ever wanted to feel more secure in your relationships? Do you regularly feel anxiety about your interactions with others? Over the last few decades, I've seen first-hand with my counseling and coaching clients that when you apply the mindset, key concepts, and tools that you will learn throughout this book, you can easily address all of these questions and more.

A Deeper Connection is based on the foundational principle that relationships are one of, if not the most important things in life. In fact, Harvard University is actively continuing the longest study ever held on happiness, which is in its eighty-fifth year. The results so far show that the people who are happiest and healthiest in life maintain relationships by being intentional about making and nurturing good ones.

Being in relationship with others is what gives us life, but it can also be challenging. Everyone faces struggles at times with how to effectively communicate their wants and needs. It can be a struggle to understand others and what they expect. Too often, difficulties in communicating lead to greater conflict, which in turn leads to feeling hurt, disconnected, and lonely.

The good news is that you are about to embark on a journey to help you live a more secure and connected life, one where you can learn to be better at relationships with others as well as develop and nurture a better relationship with yourself. You will start by learning what it means and how to develop a healthy mindset and approach to life. Then, you will learn the steps of The Confident Communication Model and how to implement it. I designed this model to help you learn how to easily address any conflict without the negative emotional impact often experienced by other approaches.

Designed to challenge ideologies and beliefs about communication and conflict, *A Deeper Connection* will serve as a guide to help you develop a healthy view-of-self, empowering you to risk vulnerability and learn to build secure relationships with others. It will help prevent the damage that happens when you respond based on your learned communication styles and automatic meaning-making. When you get angry and defensive because of your understanding of a situation, your responses often push other people away. You behave in ways that lead to the opposite of what you really want in a relationship: connection and security. Throughout this journey, you will see a new way of relating to yourself and others that can lead you to greater connection and security in all your relationships.

You will learn how to have healthier relationships by gaining an understanding of how relationships work, what conflict is, and why it exists. This includes identifying negative cycles in relationships and how they lead to escalating conflict and disconnection with others. You will learn how to stop this cycle and, instead, deal with the emotions it triggers within you.

You will start to understand and recognize that everyone has a unique lens through which they interpret the world, and you will develop your openness to others' differing lenses. The work of recognizing your meaning-making will help you to question your inner world and explore what you believe about yourself, your interactions, and the emotions you experience. Once you start to understand this inner world, you will move toward empowerment and respond to conflict in a more intentional and healthier way, instead of your automatic interpretations and the reactive emotions and actions that so often follow.

I bring a unique perspective to the topics in this book based on my varied and extensive background in mental health counseling and coaching. I am a Licensed Mental Health Counselor and have developed myself as an emotionally focused therapist and coach for individuals and couples. For decades, I have come alongside people of all ages, upbringings, ethnicities, and stages in their lives to give them hope, inspiration, and empowerment.

For a long time, I have had the desire to share with others the transformative concepts I've learned and applied in my counseling and coaching practice to help prevent people from getting stuck in the same traps I've seen time and time again. One of my hopes is that you can develop healthier ways of seeing yourself and your relationships and, for some, maybe even prevent the need for mental health therapy. I hope to offer a way to view your inner world that could decrease anxiety and depression and provide ideas for developing relationships in a way that easily addresses conflict and avoids isolation. I believe that by gaining a new way of seeing your world and how it is shaped by your thinking and beliefs, you can improve your relationships, emotional experience, and quality of life.

You, too, can learn to navigate conflict and grow your relationships, ultimately leading you to a happier, healthier, and more fulfilling life. I hope you will embrace the challenge to strive for a deeper connection with the people in your life today!

Chapter 1

REDEFINING CONFLICT

AMY IS A thirty-year-old single professional who works for a large tech firm. Her job is high-pressure, and she experiences intense stressors on a daily basis. Being a high performer, she throws herself into her work, and thanks to her competency and drive, she has been promoted quickly in the company. Amy's parents instilled in her the ideal that success meant having a great job and security, and she has held this as her own belief since she was a small child. This ideal has driven her to attain financial security and success in her career at a young age. Yet, Amy finds herself experiencing a great deal of dissatisfaction with her life.

Amy struggles with the difference between her expectations of happiness and how she feels about her life now that she has attained success. Her success has not led to the expected outcomes of happiness and fulfillment. She is stuck at a point of conflict between her beliefs and the reality of her experience, which has left her feeling stressed and dissatisfied.

One of the most pervasive and impactful experiences in our daily lives is conflict. As in Amy's case, many of us are in conflict with both ourselves and with other people constantly, whether we realize it or not. We often don't recognize the conflicts we are experiencing because, for most of us, we only recognize conflicts that reach a level of emotional impact where we cannot avoid how we feel. As we will explore in this chapter, how we view conflict often determines how we experience and respond to it.

In the following pages, I will share how many of us understand conflict and how this view negatively impacts us. An aspect of my counseling and coaching practice is working with clients to clearly develop a new working understanding of conflict that empowers each of us and provides us with the ability to address it with ease. In fact, effectively handling conflict may even result in a greater connection with others because our overall communication improves once we recognize the centrality of conflict in our relationships. I am excited to guide you through the process of developing a new understanding of conflict and an avenue to easily address conflict with confidence.

WHAT IS CONFLICT?

People often view conflict as a negative interaction in which the two parties are in disagreement. They fear that if they address conflict directly, disagreements can escalate to even greater discord. If this is the way we understand conflict, as a preface to a potentially explosive confrontation, then it becomes our expectation to have negative interactions if we disagree with others about anything. As a noun, conflict is regularly defined by its negative outcomes, such as *Webster's Dictionary's* definition of a "fight, battle, war, competitive or opposing action of incompatibles: antagonistic state or action."

Many of us anticipate a fight or battle when we address conflict, which easily sets us up to expect this as the only foreseeable outcome. If we believe conflict is a fight or battle, we go into it ready to defend ourselves rather than being open to the other person's views. If we define conflict as being antagonistic by nature, it sure doesn't feel like there is an avenue to find agreement or compatibility. When we limit our definition of conflict in this way, it leads to painful disconnection with others.

How Julie and Scott experienced conflict early on in their relationship provides a useful example for us. Julie and Scott had been dating for three years and living together for the last two. In the first few months of dating, they discussed how uncomfortable Julie was with Scott having a close friendship with Olivia, a longtime female friend. Julie had come across Scott's text messages to Olivia, which showed banter that revealed a level of intimacy that she felt was beyond what he had with her, his girlfriend. Julie knew she needed to address her feelings, and she knew it was going to get messy, so she prepared herself for a fight.

"I'm incredibly upset that you're continuing your relationship with Olivia when *I'm* your girlfriend!" she half-yelled, emotions high almost immediately. Julie didn't even give Scott a chance to interject before continuing. "The focus of your energy should be on ME, not another woman. You obviously have feelings for her, Scott; just admit it. That's why you're prioritizing your relationship with her over ours."

Without missing a beat, Scott fired back, "What are you even talking about? She's a FRIEND, Julie! I've told you time and time again. It's upsetting that you keep bringing this up and misreading my intentions."

Their fight escalated over the next couple of hours, with both defending their own position and being unwilling to hear or entertain what the other person was saying. Eventually, they both realized they were getting nowhere. In his desperation to end the argument, Scott said, "We will just need to agree to disagree."

When we make statements like "We will just need to agree to disagree," it reveals that we cannot even comprehend another way of seeing the situation. Without the right tools and insights into our differences and why we see things the way we do, we will continue to experience isolation and disconnection as thoughts and feelings are overlooked or outright dismissed. When we are disconnected, we are left feeling helpless and powerless to be in relationships with others whose views differ from ours. Ultimately, this cycle leaves many of us feeling lonely, unseen, and unloved, even in our most intimate and committed relationships.

In my practice, I encourage my clients to embrace the idea that conflict is not intrinsically bad; instead, I suggest that we simplify things and define conflict as the presence of difference. Conflict is what we experience when our differences are revealed. This definition allows us to develop an actionable approach to conflict, thus allowing us a new way of engaging one another. In fact, our differences can actually be a source of fun and joy; seeing it that way may transform our definition and beliefs about conflict itself. We can learn how to develop our ability to address conflict in more productive ways.

Our definition of conflict as difference aligns with *Webster's Dictionary's* second definition of conflict: a "mental struggle resulting from incompatible or opposing needs, drives, wishes, or external or internal demands." They also define conflict as being "different, opposed, or contradictory: to fail to be in agreement or accord." These definitions remind us that conflicts arise out of different needs, drives, wishes, and demands, all of which can feed our reactive emotions. However, here is the important part:

Just because we start from a position of disagreement does *not* mean that we need to throw our hands up and accept disagreement as the final word. This disagreement is only a representation of how differently we view our world.

In adopting this understanding of conflict, I find it important to also put "difference" into context. Just like we can define conflict as "bad," we can easily define difference as such. As I worked with Julie and Scott to explore the conflict that had ended with them agreeing to disagree, it became clear that both of them had strong interpretive lenses and they could only see the situation from their own point of view. Because of this, Julie was so frustrated that she questioned, "Are we just too different to make our relationship work?"

When discussing differences with partners, family members, or friends, I often hear clients ask the same question as Julie. If we have expectations about how another person should act in response to us, or "the right thing" to do in a situation, we can feel like difference is bad when the other person does not meet these expectations. The conflict we feel is in response to our own expectations of how the other person "should" behave; further, our defensive reaction to them keeps us from questioning our own expectations of them.

I suggest that a healthier approach is to use curiosity to understand why other people behave differently. In the situation between Julie and Scott, I used curiosity as a tool to help them explore the emotions behind what

Julie was trying to express. In this case, Julie had a deep fear that Scott really wanted to be with Olivia and not her. Without working to be curious about Julie's emotions and her interpretation, neither of them would have been able to understand what the conflict was even about. They were so stuck in using their own lenses that they couldn't even see the relational struggle that was leading them to such reactive interpretations.

The other side of this conflict was being curious about Scott's experience and the way in which his response was a defensive one. When Julie's interpretation of his thoughts and feelings didn't line up with the truth of his experience, he fought back in defense. However, once they were able to enter the position of curiosity in our sessions together, they were able to find an understanding of each other and the experience they had together. This new understanding led to them feeling a greater sense of connection and security with one another.

We each see the world differently because we make meaning of our experiences through our own unique lens. No one knows what another person is thinking or feeling without that person sharing it. Yet, often, this is *not* how we approach our differences. More often, we approach others assuming we know why they did or said something. However, because we have different interpretations, our assumptions are almost always at least somewhat incorrect, or incomplete, at the very least. Nevertheless, because we believe our assumptions are true, we cannot even recognize that our strife is of our own making, not something imposed on us by the other person.

EXPLORING THE ROOTS OF DIFFERENCE

Far too often, we overlook just how different we are from one another in terms of how we think, how we experience our world, and how we interpret those experiences. For most of us, our family's thoughts and opinions about life, expressed both verbally and non-verbally, didn't just shape our understanding but also reinforced the interpretations we carry to this day. Under these circumstances, we had constant affirmations from those closest to us that our understanding of the world was correct. Therefore, we believed that our interpretation of our experiences was just the "truth," and we failed to recognize it as an interpretation. Under these circumstances, we end up seeing our views as universally true for everyone. This inevitably leads to significant conflict when we encounter people who see things differently, which is practically everyone.

As we revisit my work with Julie and Scott, we can see how overlooking their differences was a major factor in their conflict. Julie could not understand how Scott could have a close friendship with a woman and not have feelings for her. She had never had that kind of relationship with a man or known anyone else who had that kind of relationship with someone of the opposite sex. The only thing that made sense to Julie was that there was something romantic between them. Scott, on the other hand, had seen many examples among his family and friends who were able to maintain good friendships with people of the opposite sex. It had never even crossed his mind that Julie would not see it the same way. They expected that the other person would automatically see the world as they did.

When one party holds their reality as "the reality," there is no room for the other person to productively disagree. Being stuck in this position harms relationships and, even more, it does more harm to the person stuck with this limited thinking. I describe this as a prison we make of our negative reactive emotions, which traps us in a place where we are stuck suffering in the pain of our own interpretation. If we believe our "truth" is the truth for all, we may not feel any curiosity about how anyone else thinks or feels because we think we already know. When we hold this position, we are closed off and defensive to anyone who challenges what we believe to be true.

When we recognize and value differences, we can experience freedom from needing our interpretations to be true. We can feel freedom from the emotional baggage we carry when we negatively interpret how others think or feel about us. We can engage in conflict from a position of neutrality instead of an intense emotional response. Embracing that we are all unique allows us to hold a position of openness. We no longer need our "truth" to be the truth for all, and it can open us up to a feeling of curiosity. Curiosity is the first step to truly getting to know the complex and unique nature of others and how they think and feel.

CONFLICT IS EVERYWHERE: IS THAT A BAD THING?

Every person experiences conflict on a daily basis. Why is it important for us to recognize how much conflict we face every day? Because conflict impacts us in ways that change how we feel about others, ourselves, and our experience of life itself. Too often, our negative responses lead us to amplify the conflict and the emotional impact it has on us. For example, Scott gets upset and critical of Julie for leaving dirty dishes in the sink. In response to his criticism, Julie becomes defensive. Their mutually heightened emotions escalate into a fight. They then move from his frustration with the dishes and her defensiveness to attacking each other with all their spoken and unspoken issues, which ends up leaving them in greater conflict for hours— or even days. Once we realize the pervasiveness of conflict in our lives, we can start to understand just how much our approach to conflict matters to our quality of life.

Why is conflict so constant in our lives? In addition to our conflicts with others, which I have explored above, we often also end up in conflict with ourselves. We regularly experience a negative impact from the contradictions between what we *think* is true about life and circumstances and what *proves* to be true.

Internal Conflict

The conflict we experience with others is easier to focus on than conflict within ourselves because, with others, we often move to a position of judgment and blame. We experience conflict within ourselves differently. When we have experiences that either contradict our beliefs or place us into our own definition of not being "normal," it causes intense internal conflict and distress.

Amy's experience with anxiety offers an example of internal conflict. Amy believes that having anxiety is bad because she interprets anxiety as a significant mental illness. She believes that if she is "mentally ill," she could become someone who does not have control over her actions and could cause harm to herself or her family. While it is largely acknowledged in the medical community that having anxiety itself does not lead to deteriorating mental health issues in this way, Amy interprets her anxiety differently, and that is enough to lead her into significant internal conflict.

Whenever Amy experiences any form of anxiety from the stresses of life, she becomes afraid; she cannot tolerate the emotional experience of anxiety, and she actively works to ignore and push it away. She never questions if what she believes about mental health is even true. Amy's actions end up causing her even greater distress as she becomes anxious about having anxiety, which just becomes an escalating feedback loop. As we learned earlier, Amy has a very stressful and high-pressure job. On top of that, she has been struggling with her own beliefs about the connections between mental health and success. All these factors leave Amy feeling a great deal of anxiety, and she ends up having a panic attack.

Panic attacks are bad enough, but they are made worse by Amy's misunderstood belief about mental health. Her escalated mental health issues were, in large part, being caused by her beliefs about mental health itself. She was dealing with her own internal conflict between her experience with anxiety and her interpretation of what having anxiety meant for her and her future.

Like Amy, too often, we have beliefs and ideologies that lead us to significant internal conflict and emotional distress. Yet, equally as often, we do not even recognize the beliefs leading us to have such emotional distress, much less question whether our beliefs are right to have.

We also experience significant internal conflict due to our desire to have control. Most of us don't realize the extent we go to in order to feel in control, to have answers, and to make meaning out of everything. Our meaning-making puts our experiences into a neat little box or "framework of understanding," which gives us a sense of comfort and control over our world; it doesn't feel quite so scary. Our artificial sense of control becomes a way for us to avoid living in the tension of how little we actually *do* control. We often dogmatically hold onto our framework of understanding to bring us comfort. This leads us to significant conflict with ourselves or others as we develop a strong need to prove the "truth" of our meaning-making so we can feel okay internally.

Amy's experience of defining anxiety through her own understanding of mental health is a great example of how a framework of understanding greatly affects us. She believed that she was doing great in life because she did not have any mental health issues, which meant she had to push down her anxiety. She defined mental health problems as a terrible thing for anyone to have, and she was convinced these problems would lead to terrible outcomes. She even categorized people who expressed strong emotions or could not control their behaviors as mentally ill. This left her labeling and judging others constantly and feeling good about herself in comparison, that is, until she started to experience her own anxiety. To acknowledge her anxiety would have required her to give up the control and the security that her meaning-making had created; she needed to allow herself to live in the tension of the unknown and work to redefine her understanding of mental health.

Gaslighting Experiences

When we assume we know why someone acted how they did, or they make the same assumptions about us, it is easy to quickly label this interaction as being gaslighted by the other person. According to *Webster's Dictionary*, gaslighting is:

> Psychological manipulation of a person usually over an extended period of time that causes the victim to question the validity of their own thoughts, perception of reality, or memories and typically leads to confusion, loss of confidence and self-esteem, uncertainty of one's emotional or mental stability, and a dependency on the perpetrator.

Gaslighting is difficult to spot sometimes because it can be difficult to tell when someone is trying to manipulate us into believing their version of the truth. When two individuals' understandings of an experience differ, it can leave both parties feeling like the other person is gaslighting them and telling them their truth is actually *wrong*. Both people end up feeling like their truth is being denied. We can see this as we look back at Julie and Scott's conflict over Olivia.

Julie's perspective on the issue leaves her believing that it is impossible for Scott to spend time with Olivia and not have romantic feelings toward her, which is not at all in line with Scott's truth. Because it is not his truth, he is insistent in his efforts to get her to see why she is wrong and to accept his perspective on the issue. This can leave her feeling gaslighted because she does not feel her voice is being heard. If Scott is truly gaslighting her, it seems that he is trying to psychologically manipulate her and that she is his victim. The reality of the situation is not so—instead, he is questioning her perceptions of reality because her meaning-making is not based on fact. However, in this case, if Julie applies the pathologizing label of gaslighting, she does not have to confront the source of her differences with Scott.

The more rigid and one-sided our interpretive lens is, the more we will interpret people's efforts to get us to see their perspective as gaslighting. We must be careful in differentiating whether someone is actually gaslighting us or just has a different interpretive lens about our shared experience. If we interpret the experience incorrectly, we will be unable to truly understand the other person's point of view.

The good news is that by embracing the perspective that conflict is constant and a part of being different, we can then work to adopt a new way to respond to conflict. As a result, we can create stronger relational bonds and, thus, cultivate greater and more secure attachment within our relationships.

TURNING CONFLICT INTO FREEDOM

Few people look forward to addressing conflict, as most have experienced conflict as something that does not result in good outcomes. Many of us grew up in households where behaviors were addressed, but conflict was avoided. Behaviors are just outward representations of inner conflicts. The problem is that many of us grew up with caregivers who did not have the insight, time, or energy to do more than manage our behaviors. Due to this, many of us never learned to recognize our own conflicts or those we have with others.

Most people view conflict as a confrontation about something another person has said or done. This approach to conflict will never produce a positive outcome. Even if the confrontation does not escalate into a fight, there is a good chance of damage to the relationship. When people experience this, it almost always leads to one of two defensive responses: fight or avoidance.

Who wouldn't defend themselves when someone else is demanding that they apologize for something they didn't do? In this context, I am not referring to their actions, but their intent. Yes, they may have said, "I just need to get out of here," as they left in the middle of a fight. This does not mean that they are not committed to the relationship, which the other person may believe. They may have just needed to step away and clear their head.

Often we respond without realizing how much of the fight is in response to expectations from previous experiences of conflict. Some will be quick to avoid conflict and tell the other person what they want to hear because this type of conflict is so unbearable to them; they would rather make everything feel okay than argue and be right. The main problem with these historical approaches to conflict is that even if there is "conflict resolution," there still is relational damage due to the interaction that is not addressed.

Because conflict is such a prevalent experience in our everyday lives, it has a massive impact on our moods and how we feel about others and ourselves. We do not question how we approach conflict because we simply do not know any other way. I believe it is crucial to develop a clear vision, not just about what conflict is but also about the impact our approach can have on improving our quality of life. In embracing a new vision for conflict, learning how to engage and approach conflict through a new lens can change our daily experiences dramatically.

A Place to Grow

I suggest we adopt a vision for conflict that acknowledges and embraces our differences and sees these differences as a place to grow our connection with one another. This is radically different from the need to be right we often experience when dealing with conflict. This vision moves our focus from interpreting others to being open and curious about the experiences of others and why they did or said what they did. It helps prioritize relationships and grow them with the overall goal of developing a secure attachment. In fact, conflict can lead to positive outcomes: attachment moments. The outcome of secure attachment with others impacts how safe and secure we feel in all aspects of our lives. This could lead to a genuine security that develops out of meaningful relationships, and it frees us from our futile effort to feel secure by putting our understanding of the world into a little box.

As we go down this road of working toward a new way of viewing and addressing conflict, I want to call out how transformative this process can be. It can take us from feeling like we are in a prison of emotional turmoil—bound to our own emotional interpretations and the conflict our responses create—to a place of emotional freedom, with the ability to address any conflict with confidence. We may even come to the point of recognizing how fun it can be to make meaningful and connecting interactions out of conflict through curiosity. In the next chapter, we are going to look at how this new framework can be a motivator for developing the life we really want and the factors that motivate us in our decision-making.

Chapter 2

MOTIVATION

MIKE IS A thirty-two-year-old single man who has had many romantic relationships over the last fourteen years or so, with the longest lasting nine months. His longest relationship just ended five months ago, and he is back on the dating scene. He feels incredibly lonely—which he hates—and desperately wants to find a partner to share his life with. His desperation to address his loneliness has him constantly fixated on dating apps, and he is going on dates with different women three to four times a week. The driving force for Mike to find a partner to share his life with is his motivation to no longer feel so lonely.

Motivation is *why* we do something. We all have things motivating us to act in both big and small ways throughout our days. We have motivations for why we get out of bed in the morning, where we go to work or school, why we have the job we do, why we live where we do, and why we spend time with who we do. There are motivations for every decision we make in life, yet, more often than not, we do not recognize what is motivating our decisions. Instead, we often approach life with a mindset of "this is just what we are supposed to do" or "we do what we have to." But even these statements reveal the mindset that is motivating us, even if we don't realize it.

A significant step toward empowerment is to develop our ability to *recognize* what motivates us. Once we recognize our motivations, then we will be able to choose to allow these factors to continue to impact us or choose other factors and mindsets to drive us toward the outcomes we desire.

In the following sections, we are going to explore motivation in more depth. Then we will dive into two of the most impactful motivators: the role that *fear* plays in our motivations and decisions and the influence of *hope*. Motivation can drive us toward the things we want, but it can also lead us away from hope through avoidance and self-protection. Finally, we will explore the driving force and motivation that we gain by developing a clear purpose and vision for ourselves.

WHAT IS YOUR MOTIVATION?

There are innumerable factors that motivate us to do or say the things we do. We may be motivated by the influence of our parents, mentors, friends, or faith communities. Motivation could also come in response to past experiences, which may include difficult breakups, relational traumas, or abuse of some sort. Because we are individuals, what drives or motivates us is unique to us. For example, two people may both be motivated by fear, but their differences are revealed in what they fear and how it motivates them. Other people can help us process and *discover* our motivations, but we are the only ones capable of defining our true motivations.

We can see an example of the role of motivation when we look at Scott and Julie's conflict about his friendship with Olivia. As we explored each of their individual experiences that led to their escalated conflict, it became clear that both were experiencing significant fear. Julie had a history of being cheated on by partners and struggled with trust, so when she saw texts between Scott and Olivia that she interpreted as intimate, her fear took over. She was afraid that she was not enough for him and that he would cheat on her. For Scott, hearing Julie interpret his relationship with Olivia as more than friendship triggered his own fear of being disregarded. This came in response to Julie's total dismissal of him when he disagreed with her interpretation of what he was doing and how he felt about Olivia. He grew up in a home as the youngest of three brothers, where he had felt constantly disregarded throughout his life. When Julie didn't believe him, it immediately triggered his fear and his response. In this case, both Scott and Julie were motivated by fear in different ways, but the outcome was the same in that it left each of them aggressively reacting in response to their fear.

Whether we are aware of it or not, we are motivated by the people and ideas that have influenced our development up until this point. Recognizing the factors that motivate us toward our choices is a crucial step in the process of self-empowerment on our journey to living the life we want. Without awareness of our motivators, we might stumble through life reacting to these influences without making conscious choices. Motivation is a good thing when it helps us live the life we desire but, too often, the things that motivate us are fear and self-protection, which can drive us to make choices out of self-defense versus empowerment. In other words, the more we understand our motivations, the more self-determination we exercise in our lives, and the more power we have over the person we are working to become.

Before we move on, I want you to ask yourself: Who do you want to become? What motivations will help you on your journey to becoming the person you want to be?

MOTIVATION #1: FEAR

We experience fear about issues in our lives every single day. However, we do not often categorize the issues we face as based on fear because we tend to focus on the *reactions* our fear creates, rather than the reality of the fear itself. We do not like how it feels when we think we might have a serious health issue or someone we love is dying. We do not like to feel like others believe something about us that is untrue. We do not like being misunderstood. We do not like the idea of being alone and never finding someone to share our lives with. Though it may be easy to name the ways we struggle, it is also tempting to overlook naming them as fears. Often, society does not acknowledge that our emotions are real or present in most of our interactions in life.

We experience fear more times each day than we likely realize. It shows up in concerns about how our employer views us, whether our partner loves us, if the food we eat might have allergens that will kill us, what our friends think of us, if we matter to others, if our anxiety is normal, if we are normal, if we will ever be who we want to be, and so many other things. Fear impacts our lives in innumerable ways.

We see a good example of the role of fear when we revisit Amy's belief that success means having a great job and security. She reacts strongly if a coworker or supervisor questions anything she does in her leadership role.

She has an immediate and strong defensive reaction to believing she is being judged, criticized, and called out for not being good enough. She interprets other people's simple questions to her in the workplace as a clear message that they think she is failing. Her fear of being seen as a failure leaves her reacting to these experiences by lashing out and protecting herself.

People tend to view fear as a weakness, but fear is a primary emotional experience that allows us to understand dangers and threats in our lives. Because of this, fear is a significant motivator for the choices we make in our lives. As a result of fear, we might choose to avoid going to the doctor when we think we might have cancer rather than facing a diagnosis we don't want. In this example, like many others in our lives, avoiding the things we fear does not actually make them less real or keep us from having to deal with them.

How do you understand fear, and what beliefs do you have about fear in your own life? What we believe about fear defines how we respond to it: whether we have a mindful, accepting response or one that avoids facing what our fear is telling us. If we believe it is not okay to be afraid, we tend to avoid even acknowledging the truth of our own experience of fear. If we believe that our emotions are *information* that can provide us with a greater understanding of ourselves, we will allow room for healthy acceptance of our fears. We are not afraid of fear itself, but of the meaning-making we do as a result of our fears.

Fear is not something we can necessarily remove or make better. If we fear something, there is likely a very good reason for this emotion. Our tendency is to reject fear because it feels bad to experience our feelings of it; we just want to have good feelings. When we refuse to experience the truth of our fear, we are choosing to live in denial so that we can feel better in the moment. The problem is that this does not actually make our fear go away; denial just hides it from our conscious decision-making process. We can become disconnected from our choices because we are still making our decisions in response to our fears, even though we do not allow an awareness of our fear to exist. Denial is an amazing tool our mind uses to help us through unbearable traumas, but when it comes to developing a healthy approach to deciding the person we want to be, and be that person, denial is a major barrier.

An example of how to productively engage our fear can be seen as we revisit Julie's struggle with Scott's longtime friendship with Olivia. For some time, she had struggled with her fear of their friendship, but instead of addressing her fear, she stuffed her feelings down and chose to pretend her fear did not exist. Even though she was ignoring her fear, she was still feeling it any time Olivia was part of a conversation. Although she consciously tried to ignore her fear, her body would reveal the truth as her gut would tighten, and she would immediately feel nauseous. Even though she kept telling herself she did not care about Scott's relationship with Olivia, she found herself expressing frustration and anger that was having a negative impact on her relationship with Scott. Once we finally started to work on Julie's issues with Olivia, she was able to recognize and own her fear. She was then able to both regulate her own emotional experience and have meaningful, vulnerable conversations with Scott that left her feeling more connected and secure in their relationship.

We tend to struggle with the idea of facing what we are afraid of. We define our experience of fear by how we feel about it, often without ever naming it as fear. Even our fear of *facing* fear can become the motivator that keeps us from facing the truth of our own experience. If we believe that fear is not an okay emotion to have, we deny our experience and make excuses that are more in line with our beliefs.

A significant consequence of dismissing our fear is how it impacts our relationships with others. We often do not recognize how fear impacts the ways in which we interpret what other people do or say. When our interpretation arises from fear, it closes off our openness to our differences and drives us to believe we know what others are thinking or feeling. Our lack of awareness of the role fear plays contributes to us becoming defensive, and the resulting conflict can feel disjointed and confusing for all parties involved. Fear drives a wedge in relationships and keeps us from vulnerably engaging and developing security. By developing an awareness of our own experience of fear, we provide an avenue to manage conflict with both others and ourselves.

MOTIVATION #2: HOPE

Hope is a powerful motivator that can drive us to become amazing people and do amazing things, but it also has the potential to cause us pain when we invest our hope in the wrong things. While fear motivates us because of our reaction to negative emotional experiences, hope can motivate us in a positive way that engages the possibilities of growth and change. You might even say that we are motivated to run *from* fear and *toward* hope. Since the factors that motivate us are things that stay at the forefront of our thoughts, they can set the tone for our moods and how we feel about our own lives.

Have you ever stopped to think about what hope really is? We tend to look at hope through our lens of experience and seldom think about its definition and impact on our lives. When we look at *Webster's Dictionary's* definition of hope, they describe it as "a desire accompanied by expectation of or belief in fulfillment." In this definition, hope and expectations are connected, but they are not the same thing. There is a difference between hope with expectant possibilities and just plain expectation. Hope with expectant possibilities is a hope that our expectation is possible, and possibility helps to motivate our hope. An example of this would be our hope that a family member will beat cancer. This hope drives us to move forward and fight for them, so it can drive us toward the possibilities. However, we often confuse hope with expectations. We say we have *hope* that our family member will beat cancer when we really have an *expectation* that they will, and if they do not, we fault hope for failing us.

Most of us have probably never asked ourselves if we should be putting our hope in the things we do. We go through life hoping for things we want without recognizing that what we really want may be what that object represents, not the object itself. We might hope to get a high-paying job, but perhaps it's not the job itself we want; we hope for the financial freedom the job could provide for us. I can't stress enough how important it is to be intentional about what we choose to put our hope in and be deliberate about our real desired outcome.

Dating provides many examples of hope versus expectations. In the process of dating, we can easily put our hope in wanting the relationship to work out with whoever we are with. We put our hope in this person being "the one" for us and do not recognize that our real hope might be something else entirely. Maybe we really just want to be loved and wanted by a caring partner. On a conscious level, we have focused our hope on being with the person in front of us, and by doing this, we can end up ignoring things about the person that are problematic. If we do not differentiate our true hope, we can easily miss the truth of our wants and experience. Instead of hoping and striving toward a loving partner, we settle for the person who is there.

We can see this clearly when we look at what happened in Mike's longest-term relationship with Ellen, which ended five months ago. As I mentioned at the beginning of this chapter, Mike's main motivation for being in the relationship was avoiding being alone. Until he and Ellen had started dating, he had been alone for two years. So, when he met Ellen, and she showed interest, he quickly dove into the relationship. Within the first couple weeks, he developed hope, and subsequent expectations, about Ellen being "the one" for him. He began visualizing their life together and constantly thought about their future. The first few months went smoothly, and Mike felt that Ellen liked him as much as he did her. He developed a picture of her as a loving, supportive partner who he was going to spend his life with.

Around their fourth month together, challenges began to arise in their relationship as their differences started to lead to negative interactions. Ellen had a difficult past with some significant relational trauma. She found it difficult not to interpret some of Mike's words as hostile attacks when he said something critical or even just asked her a simple question. Ellen, in turn, defended herself from what she perceived as an attack on her.

For example, Mike asked Ellen, "What are you doing?" while they sat together after dinner, each on their own phones.

Ellen would immediately snap back at him, "Can't I do anything without constantly being interrogated?"

Mike's response to Ellen's attacks was to apologize and own her interpretation of him without explaining why he asked the question. His desire to not be alone, along with the story that he had created about her being "the one," had left him working hard to justify everything through this lens.

Mike dismissed the reality of his experience and her behaviors as he tried to defend the view he had created about her and their life together that he so desperately wanted. In this, he dismissed his own feelings about what he wanted in a relationship—as long as it meant she would stay with him and he would not be alone. Mike's focus on relationships was limited to his desire not to be alone, so he had no other framework to evaluate how things were going. Mike is an example of how much our meaning-making often relies on monolithic reasoning, in which we define our reasoning through the lens of the most dominant factor. However, in reality, we often have many reasons for making the choices we do, both conscious and not. In Mike's case, he disregarded his other wants and needs for a meaningful, supportive, and loving relationship and instead settled for Ellen, who was there in front of him. He had set his hope in her just staying with him over truly being curious about who she was or evaluating whether he truly wanted her as a partner.

THE SHADOW SIDE OF HOPE

We tend to embrace hope and allow it to motivate us forward in life, or we reject and avoid it. We might reject hope because of our tendency toward self-protection, which we naturally turn to when we have been hurt or when we fear that we will be hurt. The pain we have experienced as a result of putting hope in the wrong things can easily lead us to reject hope itself. We often believe that if we don't allow ourselves to hope, then we will not feel the pain of it failing us.

When we fear getting hurt, we can take the protective position of always assuming the worst. We think that by assuming the worst outcomes in life, we can protect ourselves by never being hurt or disappointed. The tricky part of holding this position is that instead of allowing the positive life-changing value of hope to drive us forward, we are stifled by the fear of the possibility of feeling bad. In doing so, we are left in a position of feeling bad as we focus on the worst possible outcomes. We can get stuck taking on a negative outlook all the time, which significantly impacts our mood and quality of life. The reality is, no matter what position we take on hope, we get hurt if and when it fails us, no matter our stance prior to its failure. However, it hurts us more and more often when we take a position that will not allow hope to exist at all.

The pain we experience when hope fails us is real, and it can be devastating in a way that no one wants to feel. More often than not, hope fails us because we have put our hope in the wrong people or things. We can protect ourselves by not assuming the worst but instead by preventing ourselves from hoping for the wrong things. If hope has failed us, the question arises: Did we place our hope in the right thing in the first place?

Certain examples are easy to look at, such as putting our hope in a politician who lies and does not do what they said they would. But we hope in things throughout our daily lives that can be harder to recognize. We might hope that our partner will express, in meaningful ways, what we mean to them, but it never seems to happen. Too often, we hope people will respond to our needs but do nothing to express what we need or hope for from them. If our hope is that they express love for us out of nowhere, we will more often than not be disappointed. But if we hope in their ability to respond to our expression of needs, we have a much greater chance of our hopes being met.

An example of putting our hope in the wrong thing can be seen when we look at the challenges in Mike's relationship with Ellen around the fourth month. For the first few months of their relationship, things had been very good, with no noticeable conflict. For Ellen, this was affirming because she hoped that when she found the partner she was meant to be with, the relationship would naturally be easy and with very little work or conflict. However, as they entered the fourth month of the relationship and some conflict began, Ellen's hope was challenged. The conflict she experienced left her reacting with a lot of anxiety and defensiveness, which only increased the conflict between them. Ellen had an unrealistic hope that there would be no conflict—as if neither party would ever experience the ways in which they were different.

The reality, as we have explored already, is we are all different, and in so, conflict is a foregone conclusion for all relationships. Ellen put her hope in a false ideology that she would be able to find a partner with whom she had little to no conflict. However, this would require that she or her partner be so avoidant that they ignore any of their own thoughts and feelings that might clash with the other. Her choice to live in this false reality actually leads to more conflict and emotional distress. On the other hand, she could have chosen to put her hope in a different vision of the right person, hoping to find someone who would respond to her needs and address conflict in healthy ways that would leave her feeling safe and secure.

Why is it important to embrace hope as a motivator? Hope as a positive motivator is a gift. To hope is to open ourselves to the possibilities of what might be and allow positive emotions to drive us in the direction of accomplishing these possibilities. By embracing hope and making thoughtful choices about what is right for us to hope in, it can become one of the greatest motivators to accomplish our goals in life and become who we really want to be.

We have explored two of the most common motivators we deal with—fear and hope. Now we are going to explore how purpose and vision can be driving forces that intentionally motivate us toward the life we want.

PURPOSE AND VISION: THE "WHY" AND THE "WHAT"

Very few of us have ever learned the value of developing a purpose and vision. Unlike other motivating factors in our lives, the development of our own purpose and vision can be self-empowering because, in doing so, we consciously evaluate ourselves and decide what we want. There is a significant difference between purpose and vision, and by developing both aspects, we can create a clearer understanding of what we want and who we want to become. While both purpose and vision are related to goal setting, purpose focuses on the "why" of the goal, while vision focuses on the destination we are trying to reach, the "what."

For example, we can have the vision to become a doctor, but there are always other factors that motivate the vision and purpose. The purpose that drives us toward the vision of being a doctor might come out of our desire to help sick people in response to watching a family member die of cancer. Even if we do not consciously try to develop them, we still likely have a vision and purpose. Instead of coming out of a mindful process, they will likely develop as a self-protective response to factors in our lives. We see an example of this in Amy's story. She had a vision to become a high-paid executive in a position of leadership, and she worked hard to attain her goals by her late twenties. She had a clear vision of what she wanted but had difficulty describing her purpose behind it. She would often just express it as her desire not to have to rely on others.

As we spent time exploring her issues, it became clear that Amy had a difficult childhood. She grew up in a home with a lot of drug use, often moving multiple times a year and experiencing significant periods of time without any food in her home. Her childhood was unstable and chaotic, and it left her feeling incredibly insecure. She left home at fifteen years old and has been on her own ever since. Through her experiences, she had developed an understanding of the world that she could not rely on anyone else, and, in response, she took a vigilant position to never have to again. Amy discovered that her reasoning behind being in a position of power and wealth was in response to her fear and the deep level of insecurity she had experienced in her past. She never wanted to be in that position again, so she created a level of security that would never require her to rely on others. However, she never actually developed a clear vision of "what" she wanted to achieve beyond security.

Amy had unknowingly been driven by fear. Through our work together, she was able to reevaluate her purpose as being a person who would create security for others. This new, intentional purpose helped her develop a vision for the position of power she was in and guided her to work to create emotional security for the employees she managed. It also guided her in her spending, as she began to use her money to help create security for others that lacked basic needs like she did growing up. When our purpose is defined in reaction to our fears, it can drive us to focus on things that may not lead to the life we actually want.

Instead of only reacting to our struggles, we can take steps toward self-determination by first improving our mindfulness and developing a clearer understanding of ourselves and the factors that motivate us. By doing the work to recognize our current purpose and vision, we will then be able to evaluate if we want to continue holding these as our focus going forward. From there, we can thoughtfully modify them or develop a new vision and purpose of our choosing to guide us toward the future. Establishing our purpose and vision will help us to have a clear picture of who we are and what we are about, leading us to be empowered to move toward creating the life we want.

We can establish visions for many things in our lives: our careers, family, social life, or even a specific endeavor we are pursuing. Vision is a fluid thing that can be adjusted as we develop and grow. The vision we choose will have an impact on how we feel, which is why it is important that we clearly think through the vision and the possible impact it might have on us. If we establish a vision that we are going to reach a vice president title in our company by the time we are thirty-two years old, we may end up in a place of significant internal conflict the closer we get to thirty-two if we have not reached that goal.

If our vision is to be seen as a reliable and responsive worker who everyone values instead of reaching a specific title by a specific age, we would have established a goal that we can continue to strive for no matter our age. The opportunity to have positive emotional experiences significantly increases with this second example. Since work is where we spend a lot of time, a shift in perspective for our vision can have an enormous impact on our quality of life. The choices we make in establishing our vision are just as important as the effort we make to achieve it.

In the same way that establishing our vision can have a meaningful impact on our quality of life, so can our choices of purpose. If we have a vision to find a partner who could be "the one," but the purpose we establish for being in the relationship is "so that we are not alone,"—or even to "just be happy"—we will find ourselves with a huge problem. In this case, there is a disconnect between our vision and purpose because the purpose will not help us accomplish the vision. When we stop and think about it, we often realize we have a misaligned vision and purpose, which leads to a great deal of conflict both within ourselves and with others.

Looking back at Mike's experience, we can see that he had a vision of finding someone to be his partner. But he did not have clarity on the impact that his desire not to be alone would have on achieving his vision. There was nothing wrong with his vision to find a partner; the problem came out of how his purpose was in significant conflict with the vision itself. The work of developing a partnership requires a lot from both parties, but if one party is only driven by the desire to not be alone, the weakness of this purpose quickly becomes clear to the other person. We don't want to feel like we are only wanted because the other person doesn't want to be alone; we want to matter and be wanted for who we are. Mike's purpose ended up lacking the substance that would lead to successfully accomplishing the vision of partnership. In this same way, if we have a vision for developing a secure life—like Amy—and, in response, we establish a purpose that is focused on making money or reaching a certain position in society, we are likely to be sorely disappointed; in that example, we have put our expectation in things that will not provide the result we desire.

BEFORE WE MOVE ON

As we come to the end of this chapter, I hope you will take some time to look at your own life and recognize the views you hold about fear and hope and how they might be motivating you and your decisions. I also hope that you will take up the challenge of an intentional life, one that lives with a clear purpose and vision in a way that empowers you to become the person you desire to be. Our work of reflecting on how we view fear, hope, purpose, and vision is essential as we move on to understand the relational dynamics of conflict and how our motivators impact them.

Chapter 3

THE RELATIONAL DYNAMICS OF CONFLICT

THOUGH JULIE AND Scott experienced intense conflict about Scott's friendship with Olivia early on in their relationship, they were able to work through it prior to moving in together. Since then, they had what they called "normal couples' arguments" regularly, but nothing that rose to the intense level they had experienced before. As time went on, however, both Julie and Scott began to feel frustrated with their relationship as they felt their closeness slipping away. They spent most of their time together, but they both were beginning to feel disconnected from one another. Loneliness started to creep in. At this point, they sought out my support to try and repair whatever it was that was leading them to feel as if they were falling out of love.

It is common to want to be in meaningful relationships, to have good friends that support us, and to find someone we can share our lives with. Therefore, it is surprising how little effort we make to learn how to cultivate healthy relationships much of the time. It is easy to assume that all relationships are organic, that they just happen, or that we shouldn't have to invest time and energy in them. In fact, I'm sure you've heard this statement before, "When you click with someone, you just do." Many of us act as if relationships have an inevitable trajectory that is out of our control.

We can look back at any age and see the ways in which relationships were more complex than we understood at the time. As four-year-olds, we may end up in a conflict when our best friend in preschool does not want to play with us one day. As freshmen in high school, we may feel conflict when the friends that we grew up with go to another school and make new friends that they see more often than they see us; we once "clicked" with these people, but we no longer know how to navigate these relationships when things change.

Relationships give our lives meaning, whether we look through the lens of love as our core principle or just consider the logistics of survival on this planet. As we evaluate our values and needs, we can see how relationships are at the heart of everything. Relationships from birth through childhood massively form the people we become. The way we experience security or insecurity in relationships can impact our mental health and quality of life. Everyone has a deep desire to be wanted and to matter to other people; when we don't feel desired or wanted, it can significantly impact our well-being. We often respond in dysfunctional ways to others when we lack the connection we're seeking. Far too often, we overlook the significance of relationships and what they provide for us.

With all this in mind, it is quite shocking how little time we invest in becoming better at relationships. This is due, in part, to the fact that we do not know any other way to be. At other times, this is due to how little value many societies or cultures put on relationships. Often, we end up focusing on a go-it-alone attitude of independence. We are almost trained to disregard the importance of relationships. Yet the difference between bad relationships and good, secure ones is significant and impacts innumerable factors, including our enjoyment of life itself. This section will offer a deeper understanding of the relational dynamics of conflict and develop our framework to understand what is going on when we are in conflict with others.

If relationships play such a significant role in our lives, why don't we take a proactive approach to developing our ability to have healthy relationships? There may be many answers to this question, but we likely just don't know other ways to be in relationships—we just keep on doing what we've always done. In addition, too often, we assume everyone else sees the world exactly as we do. If that is the case, why would we ever think about working on something we do not recognize as an actual problem?

In reality, our differences are significant, and they lead us to a variety of ways of seeing the exact same thing. Our differences require us to step outside of our assumptions and learn how to better navigate communication with others in our relationships. By developing a new understanding of relational dynamics and ourselves, we can develop a transformative—and even freeing—approach to being in secure and meaningful relationships.

In this chapter, I want to offer a bold idea: There is hope for us when it comes to relationships. This comes in the form of developing a vision for our relationships that prioritizes secure attachment in order to create meaningful, healthy, and safe relationships. In this, we can find greater connection with others, even amid conflict. However, this process will require us to adjust our perspective and move away from automatically interpreting our relationships solely through the lens of our own experiences. We will instead need to learn to question our own meaning-making.

While developing secure relationships requires us to articulate a clear understanding of secure attachment and why it is important in our lives, it also requires that we learn how negative relational cycles happen and how they hurt relationships. We will learn to stop negative cycles and even take advantage of the conflict that leads to the cycle as a way to grow our secure attachment. Below, we will explore the importance of attachment in healthy relationships, even—and maybe even *especially*—in the face of conflict. Though the examples in this chapter that address secure attachment will be ones of intimate partner relationships, the power of secure attachment in relationships is significant in all meaningful connections, from relationships with friends to the power of a company creating a secure attachment with its employees.

ATTACHMENT STYLES: FINDING SECURITY IN RELATIONSHIPS

How do we get better at relationships? We start by evaluating our purpose and vision for them. Many of us do not already have a thought-out, clear purpose and vision, yet we likely have been working by a set of beliefs or principles that have unwittingly driven our approach to relationships. Understanding the foundational role of attachment will help us to meet our needs within relationships. By developing a vision of secure attachment and establishing the purpose of that secure attachment, we will be able to grow safe relationships in our lives and more easily address conflicts through this new lens.

Attachment has historically been viewed through the lens of those working in the area of child development. They stress the importance of children developing secure attachment because the outcome is happier children who are more socially competent and more trusting of others. Secure attachment allows children to become more stable, and they are able to manage the challenges of life with more resilience. *Webster's Dictionary* defines attachment as "a strong emotional bond that an infant forms with a caregiver (such as a mother), especially when viewed as a basis for normal emotional and social development." However, in recent years, there has been a great deal of research showing that secure attachment is not just important for children but for adults throughout our lives, especially when it comes to our primary relationships of love and support.

Attachment theory looks at humans as hard-wired for connection, and once we recognize our predictable connections to an attachment figure, we find emotional balance; in turn, this balance leads us to cultivate a grounded, positive, and integrated sense of ourselves. Doing so creates a secure foundation that enables us to succeed as we go into the world, take risks, and develop our own sense of competency and autonomy. The attributes that define secure attachment are whether the figure we're attached to is accessible, responsive, and emotionally engaged. When we are securely attached, we are comfortable with closeness and our own need for others.

There are consequences of not finding secure attachment, and they are quite powerful. If we do not find secure attachment with another person—because we see them as inaccessible, unresponsive, or threatening—we may turn to other, more *reactive* models of attachment.

The first reactive model takes the form of "anxious attachment," which comes from our sensitivity to any real or perceived negative message coming from our attachment figure. Our behaviors at this point often turn toward fighting as a way to get the attention we desire because we want to bridge the gap we're experiencing.

The second model takes the form of "deactivated avoidant response," in which we experience our loved ones as hostile or uncaring and work to get away from the conflict we are experiencing. In this case, we minimize our own needs and become fiercely self-reliant.

The third is "fearful avoidant attachment," which comes from our experience of being traumatized by one of our attachment figures. In this situation, our internal conflict is great because our loved one is the source of our fear but, paradoxically, also the solution to that same conflict. We are left in the tension between desiring their love and attention and fear of being harmed by them. This leads to significant distress in adult relationships.

The difference between how a child experiences attachment from a caregiver and how adults feel attachment is that adults experience relationships in more reciprocal ways. The importance of knowing how we experience our own attachment as adults is key to understanding ourselves and how we approach our significant others in relationships. As shown by the reactive models of attachment outlined above, when we do not have secure attachment, we develop coping tools to manage our needs and fears. Unfortunately, these coping tools are focused on our own unmet needs and do not do a good job of building relationships. These tools do not give us the connection we so deeply desire with those we love; instead, they lead to greater disconnection and feelings of loneliness. By working to develop secure attachment with others, we can both provide and receive the love and security we desire. In addition to desiring this love and security, I strongly believe that every person *deserves* those things.

FINDING ATTACHMENT MOMENTS

Our attachment style plays a major role in the way we experience and even escalate conflict in our lives. If we are not coming from a place of secure attachment, we most likely are not even sure why we react to experiences the way we do. Our attachment styles influence how quickly and strongly we react, and they often lead us to get stuck responding to one another in an escalating way, called a negative relational cycle. This catastrophic escalation of conflict leaves us feeling hopeless and alone and stuck responding to one another in defensiveness.

We can see an example of this in my work with Julie and Scott. In one of our sessions, they shared an interaction that exemplified what they called "normal couples' arguments." One day, Julie approached Scott in the living room and asked, "Did you take the garbage out?"

Scott became angry and defensive in response. He immediately lashed out at her, yelling, "Come on, Julie. I will get to it later! Why are you always so judgmental?"

At face value, Scott's response looks disjointed because he responded to a simple question from a place of fear, of which he was not aware. However, when I dug deeper into Scott's response, I discovered that he grew up in a critical home. A lifetime of experiences led him to develop a strong insecure attachment, which led him to immediately interpret Julie's question as a criticism of him. In response, Julie was left feeling attacked by Scott just for asking a simple question. She was hurt that he would interpret her intentions so negatively, and it escalated her feeling that she always needed to walk on eggshells around him.

As we can see from this example, reactive models of attachment divide us and do not help us develop meaningful relationships. The good news is that there is hope! We are not stuck with the attachment approach we have already developed; we *can* change. We have the ability to learn how to develop secure attachment with others and transform our divisive responses into connection and growth. This kind of change takes work. It is easy and even somewhat comfortable to stay in the style of relating that we have developed in response to our upbringing and experiences. But if our "natural" way of being is not secure attachment, it leaves us feeling helpless and alone in response to our relational conflict with others. While it is a challenge to change, we must keep our eyes on *why* to invest in this effort in the first place.

The transformative work of developing secure attachment helps us experience others differently and gives us the ability to address conflict in new ways. As we grow secure attachment, we will begin to address the negative cycle that starts when we get into conflict, and even learn to stop the cycle. We can turn moments of *conflict* into moments of *connection* that grow our attachment with others. We must first recognize our current attachment style and how it drives our reaction to others. Then we have to actually take the risk of learning to become someone different. It can be scary to allow ourselves to step into the unknown of change, which is why it is so important to remember that the benefits will far outweigh what is required of us.

The real question we must consider on this journey of change is: How do we grow secure attachment?

The answer is easier than we think, but first, we need to look at how we are impacted by our current relational dynamics. When we are not secure in our attachment, we can end up in constant conflict, which leaves us feeling isolated from those we love. We are quick to recognize conflict when we experience the big blowout fights that are part of our negative cycle. But this is just a part of what leaves us feeling so horrible in our relationships. In reality, our experience of separation and loneliness develops out of a culmination of moments of disconnection. All the negative encounters, looks, tones, and snippy remarks add up to an experience that is like death by a thousand little cuts. Once we feel distant and disconnected from others, it becomes easy to interpret everything they do and say as if they are against us. At this point, things really start stacking up quickly. Scott's harsh response to the question about taking out the garbage shows the cumulative effect of attachment issues on everyday experiences.

We do not grow secure attachment out of one major effort. Rather, it is the culmination of small efforts. We need to make thousands of little connecting experiences that, over time, can grow into feelings of secure connection and change. This happens in the same way that we begin to feel distant from others in the first place. We do not start feeling negative about others overnight; it is a process that depletes us before we recognize that what we feel is disconnection and unhappiness.

It can be helpful to view experiences of connection and disconnection as a balancing scale. On one side sits the weight of all the negative experiences and interpretations that leave us feeling separated from each other and can lead to feeling hopeless. On the other side are moments of attachment that leave us feeling connected, secure, safe, and in a position to see the positives about the other person. As we work toward our vision of growing our connection with others, we can see building attachment moments as a way of filling the positive side of the scale. Outweighing the disconnections can be an empowering way to seek the change we desire.

The interaction between Julie and Scott led to a good example of the simplicity of building "attachment moments." Yes, they had a challenging moment of conflict, but once they had time to calm their emotions and take down their defenses, they were able to re-engage and address their conflict. Here's how:

After a few minutes of uncomfortable silence, Scott approached Julie and took her hand gently. "I know my response was irrational, and you don't deserve to be treated that way. I don't know exactly why I'm being so reactive, but the problem is me and my reaction, not you. I am so sorry." Scott recognized that his reaction to Julie was about something he needed to figure out in himself. He also acknowledged that she did not deserve to be treated that way.

This is an attachment moment because Scott was able to be vulnerable and let Julie into his inner thinking and struggle, even though he didn't have the answers to fully understand his own behavior. He also owned his behavior and recognized that she did not deserve that treatment. Amid conflict, they developed a more meaningful connection and a deeper relationship because of the work they were doing to understand themselves and each other.

Even if we recognize that this work takes place in small increments, change is hard. We might not feel very motivated to do the work to save and strengthen our relationships on a daily basis because of how disconnected and hopeless we may feel. The reality is, if we don't do the work, we are going to end up experiencing this same dynamic with others indefinitely because we are responsible for our disconnection with the other person. The only way to really change our negative experiences is to recognize and respond to our experiences of conflict.

Secure attachment is the culmination of moments of connection that we develop with each other. Connection moments can be big *or* small, but the power they hold is cumulative. Connection moments can consist of sharing how your day went with a partner and feeling the connection of them caring about you. It can be a kind expression about how much someone means to you. It can be holding hands with a loved one while going on a walk. It can be crying with another while they are hurting from a loss. It can be owning and apologizing for our behaviors when we hurt someone. It can be sharing our thoughts and feelings. There are so many ways for us to have connecting moments that build our attachment that, in fact, we can easily see opportunities for attachment when we are purposeful about it. Secure attachment allows us to express our love in relationships and build something solid and secure.

THE NEGATIVE COMMUNICATION CYCLE

One of the greatest challenges we have regarding relationships, and our ability to develop secure attachment, is our struggle to communicate well. These struggles can lead to increased conflict and disconnection from one another. The factor that often leads to this disconnection is what is called the negative cycle. The negative cycle can happen in any relationship and likely has happened in most of ours. It is the experience of conflict in which we participate in a back-and-forth escalation of emotionally reactive responses. Our responses are not about what the other person is saying as much as how we are *experiencing the other person* in that moment of interaction.

In this situation, we have a strong emotional response to the words of the other person, which triggers our defensiveness. Instead of addressing—or even realizing—what actually triggered our response, we usually focus on our defensiveness. In turn, the other person is also having a similar experience, reacting to our defensive energy. Likewise, the other person does not recognize that their defensive reaction was based on *how* we said something. This is the main problem with the cycle: it exists in the subtext of what is happening, but our awareness usually never leaves the subject that is being discussed.

The negative cycle has a great impact on our efforts to develop secure attachment. If our vision for developing a meaningful relationship is to create a secure attachment, then the negative cycle is our enemy in this effort. The outcome of the negative cycle is disconnection with others. The individual moment of disconnection that we feel after a cycle is painful, but the real negative power is produced through the culmination of cycle after cycle and moment after moment of disconnection. This leads us to an experience of feeling incredibly separate from the other person. We are left with a deep feeling of loneliness, even though we might be spending all our time with this person.

The culmination of negative disconnection creates a massive divide that can cause us to feel hopeless about our relationships. What is so insidious about the cycle is how it drives us deeper into conflict. We can end up saying and doing things that we normally never would as a response to our desire to escape the trap of the negative cycle we are in. This tends to lead to significant relational injuries as it continues to happen over and over again.

In the negative cycle, the person who initially shares their frustration will react negatively to the other's defensive posture, which arises in response to *how* they shared their frustrations. In turn, the defensive party will react to the initial person's own defensiveness. On and on it goes, each person reacting to the other's reactions. Most of the time, one or both parties will be working to stay on the original topic of discussion, but most of us do not recognize the underlying experience that is moving our conflict forward. In the end, the negative cycle can be summed up as an escalating reaction to each other's reactions. This reaction is not just to *what* is said but also to non-verbal signals such as body language, tone, and volume. Next, we will look at how to recognize this cycle, which is the first step to breaking the cycle.

How Did We Get Here?

The real challenge in breaking the negative cycle is to develop our ability to recognize the cycle as it's happening. For most of us, the cycle is an unconscious process that has been taking place all our lives. However, we can struggle to see its presence when it is happening. A simple way to recognize that the negative cycle has taken place is when we hear the statement, "How did we get here?" after arguing for an extended period.

An example of the negative cycle can be seen through another conflict between Julie and Scott. Julie is frustrated with how Scott loads the dishwasher. "You're still not loading the dishwasher right. I am constantly re-cleaning the dishes after a wash that you loaded, and you waste water by only loading about half as many dishes as I do," she says, angrily re-distributing the dishes while he stands helplessly.

They have had this discussion many times since moving in together, and she is upset and frustrated by it. Her tone *and* words make this abundantly clear. He hears her criticism and responds defensively by saying, "Well, the one and *only* time you have ever cleaned out the cat's litter box, you left a mess that I had to clean up. I'm always the one who has to take care of the cat."

Getting even more heated, Julie fires back, "Before we lived together, you were so sweet and treated me like a princess. Now, you just criticize me and don't show me the love you once did."

After an hour and a half of going back and forth—criticizing, judging, and at times getting angry and yelling at each other—they break down in exhaustion. Scott finally says, "What are we even fighting about? How did we get here?"

Julie and Scott feel exhausted, overwhelmed, and frustrated, and they do not want to be around each other. As the conversation ends, they head to separate spaces and simply exist in the same house for the next couple of days, interacting and speaking at a bare minimum and feeling the ongoing tension of their disconnection. After a few days, Scott takes a risk and tries some playful banter with Julie. Luckily, it breaks the ice, and she also begins to re-engage in a way that is normal for their relationship. Julie and Scott, like most of us, do not recognize their negative cycle and what has happened. They just feel the pain of the conflict and judge the other person for hurting them.

Like Julie and Scott, many of us get into fights that start with one person upset about one thing and end with both parties arguing about countless issues until both are frustrated, angry, and exhausted. When we are feeling threatened, our response is to feel defensive. We put up walls and take a "fight-or-flight" position to defend ourselves. This escalates one person's frustration into a negative cycle, and it often occurs within a split second. It is important to understand that both parties are fully responsible for the negative cycle. Both play an active role in its creation and continuation; even if we think we can define where the cycle started, we are likely wrong. This is because the cycle did not just start at one exact moment.

Our reactive and defensive responses are likely connected to many other issues that have happened in the relationship in the past and may even be connected to past relational injuries with others.

It's hard to learn about negative cycles and our role within them because we often do not even know they exist. Developing our mindfulness and teaching ourselves to recognize and stop the cycle is the first step, and it necessitates effort. Just like going to the gym for the first time, it requires us to build new muscles, which is challenging and difficult until we really find our groove. Once we start to understand our cycle and how we move within it, these cycles are actually not that difficult to spot.

First, we can become mindful of our emotional reactions to others. If we recognize ourselves feeling reactive emotions such as frustration or anger, this is a clear sign that the cycle is alive. If we are expressing these feelings, we are playing an active role in escalating the cycle.

Another way to recognize the cycle is by paying attention to how we feel in our body, which is the physical manifestation of our emotions. An example of this might be when we feel our gut dropping or tension in our shoulders or neck. How we experience the physical manifestation of our emotions can look different for every person, but we all tend to experience our emotions through physical sensations before we recognize them on a conscious level. This becomes a useful tool to recognize the cycle's presence quickly.

Another quick recognition of the cycle can be our own internal desire to escape a conversation. If we experience the tension of not wanting to have the conversation, we are picking up on our own internal reaction to whatever is happening. This reaction is a part of the cycle and will lead us to reactive behaviors that will likely escalate the cycle.

Another clear marker that the cycle is alive in us is if we are experiencing defensiveness and want to protect ourselves.

We can also recognize the negative cycle coming alive by paying attention to the other person's stories, body language, emotional expressions, and energy. Too often, we ignore the body language of other people, but we should see it as clear evidence that the cycle is alive when the person's look or posture is defensive, angry, or irritated.

Another way to recognize the cycle is alive is by paying attention to how we are experiencing a shift of energy. We can be having a fine conversation and, all of a sudden, we can sense something has just happened and it is coming from them. By paying attention to the markers that help us recognize the cycle, we now have the ability to see it and work to stop it.

As I worked with Julie and Scott, I was able to help them recognize the negative cycle they were in. I did this by helping them see how quickly they had gone from a conversation about loading the dishes to one in which both were just reacting. As Scott felt judged and criticized by Julie, his defensive wall went up, and he felt attacked. He worked to defend himself and to diminish the fear he was feeling about her criticism of him. He desperately wanted her to see how wrong her interpretation of him was.

In response to his reactive and defensive approach, Julie also moved into a position of reaction, and her own defensive wall went up. She worked to protect herself against what she perceived as an attack from him. She also worked hard to get him to see her perspective. Ultimately, they both were left yelling at each other while not allowing the other to hear what they were trying to say. They were stuck reacting to the other person's reactions as the argument just continued to escalate.

Recognizing the negative cycle is easier when we are in a moment of direct conflict and experiencing defensiveness. It is harder to recognize the ways in which the cycle might continue after the main conflict appears to be over. The cycle can carry on for hours, days, or even weeks. It might not end at all because we do not understand what happened in the first place. We are still reacting to the story that our experience of the cycle created about them and their actions, but understanding and addressing what has actually happened is another matter entirely. Because of this, we can be left pausing and restarting the negative cycle and magnifying the disconnection over an extended period.

We desperately want the other person to hear and see our truth, but we end up screaming at a brick wall. Until each person de-escalates and takes their defensive wall down, we will not be able to find a meaningful connection. Defensiveness demonstrates the futility of continuing to argue—or even trying to get our point across when the cycle is alive—because it is not fertile ground for connection. Our defensiveness will only lead to greater relational conflict, trauma, and disconnection.

Are You a Pursuer or a Withdrawer?

As we work to understand our own experience of the negative cycle, it is important to recognize that often one of us takes on the role of a pursuer and the other that of a withdrawer. The pursuer has the drive to pursue the other for a resolution to the conflict immediately. The idea of leaving the argument without resolution is unbearable and creates a great deal of anxiety for them. The pursuer desperately wants to feel secure with the other person in the moment, and the idea of living in limbo about how the other views them is intolerable and drives them to aggressively pursue a resolution in the moment.

In contrast, the withdrawer has a need for space and time. They often take time to process, and they get overwhelmed by conflict and struggle; they need to take time alone to make sense of the conflict, wanting to escape it as soon as possible. For them, the idea of continuing a negative engagement is unbearable and causes them great anxiety and distress. They need space but cannot get it because of the demands of the pursuer.

As we look back at the negative cycle Julie and Scott experienced about loading dishes, the pursuer/withdrawer dynamic was something we were able to clearly see escalating the cycle. In our previous work together, we had established that Julie was a pursuer and deeply wanted a resolution to the conflict at the moment it was happening. Scott, on the other hand, was a withdrawer and needed space when there was conflict so he could organize his disjointed thoughts. It became clear in our work that their positions of pursuer and withdrawer had escalated their negative cycle to the point of significant disconnection. As the conflict continued past the first few rounds of back and forth, Scott shut down and felt overwhelmed by the confusion of the experience, unable to make sense of what was actually going on. He wanted to escape and thus clammed up while Julie kept going.

When Julie saw Scott shutting down, she had a strong emotional reaction. She had a deep fear of abandonment, and seeing him disengage from the conversation led her to pursue him and a resolution even more aggressively. She did not want them to leave this conversation unresolved. As she escalated her pursuit, Scott was more overwhelmed and shut down even more, which, in turn, caused her to get louder and more aggressive. Eventually, Scott hit a breaking point. He could not tolerate the conversation any longer; he went from complete shutdown to attacking her in an effort to get her to stop her pursuit so he could get unstuck. It worked, and Julie was so hurt and afraid of his reaction that she stopped and stormed out to get away from him.

The challenge with the pursuer/withdrawer dynamic is that each position escalates the other person's response simply because of their own desire not to feel the impacts of the other's position. Each of these positions immediately threatens the other's needs. The withdrawer feels overwhelmed by the pursuer's aggressive pursuit and, in turn, shuts down and escapes internally even more. This leaves the pursuer feeling abandoned by the withdrawer, which increases their conflict anxiety and escalates their pursuit. The feeling of being stuck in the cycle quickly intensifies in a way that can be unbearable. This escalation can lead us to do and say horrible things in an effort to shut the other person down and escape their cyclical behaviors.

However, we need to remember that *we* are the only ones responsible for *our* behaviors. Even when we understand what leads to our harmful behaviors and how we may not be speaking our truth, we still need to take responsibility for our hurtful words and actions and own what we have done. The person experiencing our aggression can only see that we have acted out, and they feel injured by our words or actions. Our bad behaviors can create a vision of who we are to others that is only accurate in the context of the cycle. We need to simultaneously work to build a vision of the person we *aspire* to be as well.

The dynamics that happen in a negative cycle are not always pursuer/withdrawer; they can also be pursuer/pursuer or withdrawer/withdrawer. Each pairing has its own complications. The pursuer/pursuer has both parties aggressively pursuing a resolution, and both are left aggressively stuck in their own positions, trying to get each other to hear their perspective and yelling at the other person's defensive wall. In contrast, the withdrawer/withdrawer dynamic can make it seem like a negative cycle never happens. Both parties are often so avoidant as to never directly address any conflict they are feeling. For them, it becomes an unspoken cycle of conflict that never gets addressed because of their unwillingness to engage. Instead of leading to a huge blowout, their positions as withdrawers can lead to them feeling extremely disconnected for the sake of keeping the peace. Active participation in a negative cycle will lead us to feel hurt and disconnected by the other person's words and actions, no matter which position we take.

During our negative cycle conflicts, we easily forget the most important fact: the other person is someone we care about and value. It is a natural response to feel like the other person is our enemy. However, once we understand that the negative cycle is our real enemy, we start to realize how it is attacking our attachment and the safety and security that attachment can offer. We must recognize that the real enemy in our battle is the negative cycle itself, our common enemy, and we can learn to work together to fight for connection.

Outcomes of the Conflict Cycle

The most predictable thing about a negative cycle is its outcome. If we do nothing to stop a negative cycle, we can be assured that we'll end up feeling disconnected from the other person. The long-term impact of the negative cycle is that we feel distant, disconnected, and alone even when we may constantly be in the presence of the other person. The negative cycle erodes attachment, leaving us feeling insecure about our relationships and detached from others. Often this result can be seen when people make statements like "Maybe we just aren't right for each other," "I'm just not in love with you anymore," or "Maybe we are just too different to be friends."

The negative cycle can also cause others to tell a story about who we are due to the destructive behaviors they witnessed during our negative cycles. We are judged by the worst part of us that showed up during the cycle. The negative cycle also impacts how we view and experience others in these same ways. We are left viewing others with a skewed perspective of who they are and why they are behaving badly, which can have a significant impact on our own mental and emotional well-being. As we see what the negative cycle is and how destructive it is to relationships, we begin to understand the importance of learning to stop it. A powerful motivator in doing so is our desire to be seen by others and to see them for who they really are and no longer allow the cycle to negatively define us.

On the other hand, the outcome of stopping our negative cycles is also very predictable. We are stopping an enemy that produces only division, fear, and pain. By doing so, we create opportunities for connection instead of division, and we grow from our differences—differences that are inherently part of every relationship we have. We have the opportunity to move toward growing our connections with others by creating attachment moments that tip the scale to the side of secure attachment and all it has to offer. In doing so, we choose a road that builds versus tears apart. Stopping the negative cycle starts with the process of recognizing it because we know that no good will be produced by engaging in it. We can embrace a new vision of ourselves free from the bad behaviors the cycle has produced in us—a new vision with confidence in who we are becoming.

KNOW YOUR ENEMY

As shown throughout this chapter, relationships are a major part of our lives. We can gain a new understanding of the relational dynamics that lead to conflict and embrace this transformative approach to growing secure and meaningful relationships. We have come to see how we should strive for a secure, attached relationship, and we have explored the importance of knowing our attachment styles and how they impact our reactions to others. We have also worked to develop a clear understanding of the negative cycle in our relationships and how it should be viewed: the cycle is the enemy, not the person we experience conflict with. Once we develop these understandings as part of how we view our relationships and interactions within them, we have a new framework to address the conflicts that arise.

As we move forward in our effort to learn how to address conflict, we must begin by changing our own framework to see the dynamics at play in a new way. The next step will be developing our understanding of how emotions play into our conflict, and in doing so, we will see why we react in ways that feed the negative cycles we experience.

Chapter 4

RESPONDING TO EMOTIONS

SARA IS A thirty-five-year-old married mother of two who experienced a sexual assault while dating a man when she was twenty-three. Soon after the assault, she began counseling with a therapist who really helped her work through her trauma. While working with that therapist for three years, she was able to deal with her assault and grow, learning how to be in healthy relationships in a way that ultimately led her to a happy and secure marriage with Brian. She had a tremendous amount of gratitude for her therapist and all he did for her. In fact, she viewed their experience together as a big part of her healing that allowed her to become the person she is today.

Sara came to me as a client when she unfortunately discovered that her former therapist—the person who had helped her process her own trauma so much—was just arrested for sexually assaulting a woman he was dating. Discovering these claims against him left Sara distraught. She immediately started to question the truth of her own experience and the narrative she had constructed during their three years of working together. She struggled to make sense of how a person who had helped her could do to another woman what she had vulnerably shared in such painful detail.

Sara was unable to make sense of her feelings about the new accusations against her therapist. What he had done was horrific and evil in her eyes. Yet her own experience had led her to view him as a guardian angel who worked with her to overcome her pain and begin to heal. Sara did not feel okay having any emotions besides hatred and disdain for what her therapist did to this woman.

Too often, we get stuck in our need to make meaning out of what has happened, and sometimes we just cannot. In reality, our world is one of emotional paradox. We go through each day experiencing the full range of our emotions. Some of these contradictory emotions exist in the same space and time, just as they did for Sara. She hated her therapist for what he did to another woman and felt gratitude for what he did for her. Both are true at the same time.

Emotions are complex by their very nature. They are made even more complex by a society that does not put much value on them. We tend to look at our world in very black-and-white terms when it comes to how we feel or "should feel." Our idea that there are "wrong" emotions ends up defining our experiences in very limiting ways. It is easy for us to develop a simplistic position about someone based on one thing they did that feels incredibly wrong; often, we then disregard the rest of who they are and what they have meant to us or done for us.

Emotions lead to conflict, but not because of the emotions themselves. The conflict comes from our *beliefs* about emotions. When we believe emotions are a problem, we work to avoid them, which can have a negative impact on us. When we believe it is wrong to have specific emotions and then we experience them, we can turn against ourselves for experiencing what we think we should not. We can even start to see ourselves as broken, failing, or not capable of what we believe everyone else can do. *Everyone else can manage their emotions; why can't I?*

We may not even recognize our beliefs about emotions, which can also be problematic. We can lack awareness of why we believe what we do.

We now want to explore emotions and their role in the conflicts we experience. We will explore how we view and react to emotions and how each of these can escalate the conflicts we experience. We will also differentiate primary and reactive emotions and learn to evaluate our relationships for emotional safety while learning how to self-regulate our own emotional experiences.

EMOTIONS:
TO BE EMBRACED, NOT FEARED

The messages we received from our caregivers as we grew up shaped how we experienced our world; from them, we learned what to define as right or wrong, good or bad. Many of us grew up in homes where we received two main messages about emotions: "You are too emotional" or "Emotions are not okay." We likely received these types of messages both directly and indirectly with statements such as "I will give you something to cry about" or just being told to "stop crying" when expressing emotions. Through these experiences, we end up believing that our emotions are not good and that it is unacceptable to express them or even experience them.

The hypocrisy is that in the midst of messages that emotions are not okay, there seems to be one exception: anger. People are not comfortable with us expressing what they would call "difficult emotions," like fear and sadness. Yet our caregivers and others often seem to have no problem expressing their own emotion of anger at our tears, even if the tears may be in response to how we are experiencing their anger. If we express our emotions of sadness or fear, it is often quickly judged as weakness—something we are wrong to express. Yet if something goes wrong, people have no problem getting angry and yelling. Anger is somehow a more acceptable emotional response, perhaps given its association with strength.

When we live among people who reject emotions, we are left completely out of tune with our own emotional experiences. There is a cognitive dissonance when we have emotional experiences because we have been trained to disregard or reject them as unacceptable. This dissonance leaves us living in denial about the truth of our experiences. Because we avoid our own emotional experiences, we avoid mindfulness about what we think and feel; we are left viewing our world through a reactive lens that does not even recognize the filters we are using for interpretation.

Denying our emotions is like denying we have limbs. Our arms and legs are a part of us as we go about living our lives, and we will stumble or flail every time we move if we do not recognize they are hanging off our bodies and manage them correctly. The same is true for our emotions.

Society has cultivated a skewed perspective of strength and weakness. The idea that we are weak when we express emotions might come from our fear of recognizing our own emotions. However, it actually takes immense strength to embrace our emotions in a culture that constantly says not to. Many emotions, such as sadness, fear, and anxiety, are not enjoyable to experience. It could also be said that we do not like emotions because of the unpredictable nature of how we have experienced them within ourselves and in interactions with others. By continuing to reject the truth of our emotional experiences, emotions will continue to show themselves in unpredictable and offensive ways. I want you to know that it does not have to be this way.

If we believe our own emotions are unacceptable, we are left with a great deal of internal conflict when we inevitably end up experiencing them. This can lead to much more challenging mental and emotional issues than if we had just accepted them as okay. An example of this can be seen as we revisit the story of Amy, who believed that having anxiety was bad. In fact, Amy believed that if she experienced anxiety, she could end up hurting herself or others she loved, which she was deathly afraid of. She had a negative belief that people who struggle with anxiety are weak or broken in a way that will escalate to greater mental health issues, including the loss of their ability to control themselves.

Amy's belief had a significant effect on her as a young woman when she choked while eating, which led her to be afraid of choking again. This, in turn, caused her to have anxiety about her fear of choking. She was able to overlook the impacts of her anxiety, even though it caused her mental distress for years. The real problem began when she became an adult and started feeling the pressures of responsibilities and a loss of control. Amy began to experience extreme anxiety, to the point of having a panic attack. At this point, her negative belief about emotions moved from the anxiety itself to a compounded anxiety due to her beliefs about *what it meant* to have anxiety. She went from a normal experience of anxiety to a complicated experience of having anxiety about anxiety itself.

Amy's belief that her anxiety was bad created a feedback loop that became debilitating because her mind continued to race in an effort to *try* to make sense of it; in turn, this led to more anxiety as she constantly thought about her anxiety. All her efforts to overcome anxiety came from a desire to control how she felt. She struggled to realize that how she felt came out of her *beliefs* and that everything would have felt different if she had made peace with her anxiety in the first place.

Emotions are one of the most direct ways we have to learn to understand ourselves. They can allow us to understand how we feel, and if we are mindful, they can lead us to the "why" of what we are believing and reacting to. Emotions are the gateway to our inner world and, ultimately, our own ability to choose what we believe and how we want to react to life.

As we explored Amy's struggle with anxiety, we discovered her deep fear of not having control over her life. Her desire for control was driving her to reject her feelings of anxiety. Thus, she worked to have control over her feelings instead of allowing them to provide information about her thoughts and beliefs that led her to feel this way in the first place. By understanding what led to her feelings of anxiety, she could be empowered to choose what she wanted to believe going forward, thus impacting how she would feel in response.

In addition to letting us understand ourselves better, emotions can serve another purpose: to understand *others* better. In the same way that emotions are information we can gain for ourselves, they are information about other people's experiences. By learning about the importance and dynamics of how emotions play out in our lives, we can gain a new understanding of others that changes how we view them. Through this process of embracing emotions, we can go from reacting to someone's anger or frustration to seeing anger and frustration as reactive and not the truth of what is going on for them. When we interpret anger and frustration as a reaction to a primary emotion, it changes us and how we respond to them. We no longer need to defend ourselves but instead can learn to tune into our empathy and curiosity about our differences, knowing that others do not see the world the same as we do. We'll explore more about this and primary emotions later on.

Because we have come from a culture that has largely taught us to reject emotions, the work of learning to embrace emotions is a challenge. It requires us to *choose* to believe something contrary to what we have been taught. It takes strength to stop being afraid of our own emotions and embrace them as a necessary and valuable part of who we are. By doing so, we no longer need to deny an essential part of ourselves. We need to learn to embrace our emotions and start to see them as the truth of our experience and the best way to really know ourselves. Embracing our emotions and integrating them into our lives provides us with a gift: to be free in our emotional experience and no longer be bound to the negative impacts of our emotional ignorance.

PRIMARY VERSUS REACTIVE EMOTIONS

As we work to recognize the role emotions play in our experience of conflict, we must clearly define the difference between primary and reactive emotions. Making this distinction will allow us to develop a new framework for how we reflect on our own emotional experiences, as well as our emotional interactions with others. Differentiating emotions allows us to more clearly understand the dynamics that have naturally been happening in our conflicts. We are empowered to take ownership of our emotional experiences, which lays the groundwork to *choose* our emotional response rather than being driven by our reactive emotions.

Reactive emotions include anger, jealousy, resentment, and frustration. They occur as a reaction to our primary emotional experiences, and they are the easiest feelings for us to recognize. In our world, these are often the acceptable emotions to have, the emotions that people think show strength or empowerment. In reality, they come alive to protect and defend us from how we really feel on a primary level.

Primary emotions are defined as the deeper, more vulnerable emotions of fear, sadness, hurt, loneliness, and shame. These emotions are harder for us to recognize because they are usually overshadowed by the reactive emotions that come alive in defense of them. These are emotions that are full of vulnerability, and our culture tends to portray them as a weakness. But it takes a great deal of strength to be vulnerable and risk acknowledging our primary emotions than the protective stance of reactive ones that only work to defend us.

If we call what scares us a *weakness*, then we can consider ourselves strong and justified in being defensive and staying in our reactive place. This is how our mind rationalizes the protective stances we take, but it does not make it true. It leaves us defending and protecting ourselves from the things we are afraid of under the guise of calling this protection *strength*.

The most common primary emotion we experience is fear. Aside from fear, we usually feel sadness, hurt, or loneliness. Experiencing shame as our primary emotion is rare. It does not matter which of the five primary emotions we experience—fear, sadness, hurt, loneliness, or shame—they are all the true emotions of our experience.

The interplay between primary and reactive emotions is challenging because we have learned to be much more comfortable with our reactive ones. This, in turn, hides our awareness from those emotions that are primary to our experience. An example of this is the way we experience anger. Once our anger locks in, the story about what a person did and how they hurt us grows. We are stuck in our anger until it dissipates, but the damage and disconnection are done. If we come to understand that our reactive emotions are not the truth of our experience, we can shift out of anger as we work to recognize the truth of our primary emotion. Once we recognize that our anger arose in defense of our fear, we can acknowledge the fear itself as a way to grow our connection. Expressing primary emotions grows connection, while expressing reactive emotions destroys connection.

Many of us fear our fear. We interpret being afraid as a weakness, and we are not okay with it. In reality, fear is prevalent in all of our lives. If we look at the major themes of people's struggles—in movies, books, or stories in general—we can notice that fear is actually a main character. It is often not even referred to as fear; instead, we call it "cheating death" or the underdog finding love. Even in how we discuss fear, we struggle to name the reality of the fear we are experiencing. We often express messages about overcoming the challenges of our fear.

Tuning into our primary emotions gives us the ability to move out of our reactive experience into what is foundationally true to our experience. By doing so, we grow our awareness of the reactive dynamics that feed negative cycles in our lives. We also encounter an off-ramp from the dead-end of our reactive emotions, such as anger. We no longer have to be stuck in our anger and the suffering it brings. We can step out of it into our primary emotion, which allows us to approach others with vulnerability versus the defensive stance of our reactiveness. We can realize that our reactive emotions keep us locked in a mental and emotional prison of reacting to others, while our primary emotions are the key to our mental and emotional freedom from this prison.

A NEW KIND OF FACT CHECK

We often do not recognize the dishonesty of what our reactive emotions communicate to us because our experience of them feels so true in the moment. We believe that "emotions are emotions," and we treat them as if what they are telling us is straightforward. As we begin to learn about the differences between reactive and primary emotions and their significantly different roles in our emotional experience, we start to recognize that they are not "just emotions."

We have likely gone through life thinking little about emotions and their role. This has left us automatically responding to experiences and whatever feelings show up for us. We seldom question the factors that lead us to feel the way we do. Yet our emotions can affect us in detrimental ways in terms of how we engage in relationships as well as our own inner world. Now that we have developed an understanding of the difference between reactive and primary emotions, we have a foundation to begin to understand and learn to manage our own emotional experiences in a way that can bring us improved mental well-being and an increased ability to navigate relationships and conflict more positively.

In the process of learning to understand and manage our emotional experience, it is crucial that we learn the value of our primary emotions. For reference, primary emotions show up in the form of fear, sadness, hurt, loneliness, and shame. However, even if we are feeling one of these emotions, it is not automatically a primary emotion. It is primary when we can recognize it is a core emotion we are experiencing for a specific situation within a relational context. For example, having a fear of spiders is not a primary emotion, while the fear that someone will abandon us *is* a primary emotion. Primary emotions provide a framework for our process of self-discovery about how we relate to people in our lives, including ourselves. We discover our primary emotion as we tune into our own emotional experiences and look to understand the differences between our primary emotion and the reactive and defensive emotional experience it triggers.

Locating our primary emotion is actually much easier than it seems. It starts with our ability to realize that we are in a negative cycle or, even more simply, that we are feeling reactive to whatever is happening. If we are experiencing anger, jealousy, resentment, and frustration, we are in the midst of reactive emotions. Once we recognize these reactive positions, then we turn to discover the primary emotion behind our reactive defensiveness. Checking our primary emotion is easy because we are only looking at five specific emotions. The primary emotion that is alive most of the time is fear, which makes it the first place we should check with ourselves. If we do not see fear as our primary emotion, then we should check if we are experiencing sadness, hurt, or loneliness. The least likely primary emotion is shame, which is normally experienced as a reactive emotion in which we think something is inherently wrong or flawed with us at the core. Though on the rarest occasion, it can be primary, most people will not experience it as such.

As we recognize we are experiencing reactive emotions and work to discover our primary emotion, we should first ask ourselves: What am I afraid of? If it is not fear, we can move on to ask: Am I feeling sad, hurt, or lonely about what I am reacting to?

The result of understanding our primary emotion is that it leads us to self-regulation, which can grow our ability to address conflict without escalating it. Self-regulation is important because, without it, we will just continue to automatically feed the reactive emotions we feel. When we learn to approach relationships by vulnerably sharing our primary emotion, it invites the other person to respond to our needs and creates connection, leading to secure attachment. It invites the other into our struggle and sets them up to respond empathetically.

Let's take Sara and Brian, for example. Brian tells Sara that he made plans with some friends, but he didn't ask Sara before he told them yes. In previous instances, Sara would have been frustrated and upset, half-shouting, "How could you do that? You are so thoughtless. You obviously do not care about me; otherwise, you would have talked to me before making plans!"

However, this time, Sara takes a step back and realizes there is a primary emotion at play. She calmly says, "Your action brings up a feeling of fear that you don't care enough about me or want to discuss plans before making your own decisions. I don't know what to do with my fear that this might be true." In this instance, Sara focuses the discussion on her own primary emotion of fear and asks for his help addressing her fear.

Inviting others into our needs stands in stark contrast to how we often respond to others with our reactive emotions. Normally, we interpret our experiences and then share these negative interpretations as defensive stories that criticize and judge the other's thoughts or behaviors. This causes disconnection and damages relationships. Thus, it is challenging to develop a new way of seeing our emotions and learning to respond to them. The good news is that it gets easier and easier to tune into primary emotions once we start down this path. Once we have developed a clear picture of even just one primary emotion, we have an easy first step to checking what our emotions are really about when we experience reactiveness in the future.

ARE THEY SAFE?

When utilizing our primary emotion to address conflict, we should first evaluate how safe it is to address our conflict with that person. By safe, I mean, are they emotionally safe for us to share our thoughts and feelings with? Or do we already know of factors that make them unsafe for us? We should not blindly jump into addressing conflict the same way with everyone in our lives because it may not be appropriate to approach some relationships with a deep level of vulnerability.

One facet that can allow us to determine our level of safety with someone is simply defined by the role they play in our life. There is a difference between the type of safety we may experience in relation to an intimate partner, family member, or friend versus a co-worker, manager, or stranger in the community. This is not to say that a partner or family member is automatically safe. But it is far more likely that we will see family or friends as safe for us than we would, or even maybe should, a co-worker or manager. Once we recognize if the relationship is safe, we are left to evaluate to which degree the individual is safe to share our thoughts and feelings with. This will determine how to address the conflict we are experiencing.

Evaluating the safety of an individual should take into account whether that person has the emotional intelligence and the ability to hear and take in what we would be vulnerably sharing with them. One way to understand this is by analyzing if they can see our perspective or if the lens through which they see the world is the only lens that exists for them. Do they believe that if someone sees things differently, they are just wrong? The last thing we want to do is express vulnerability to someone who is unsafe because they will not have the capacity to connect to our vulnerability. Instead, we will likely be crushed by their response to it.

In our process of evaluating for safety, it is also essential that we decide whether now is the time to address the conflict. We should not just evaluate if someone is an emotionally safe person. Are they emotionally safe for us *in this moment* when we are looking to address the conflict? Just because someone normally falls in our category of trust and safety does not mean they are safe when they are being reactive to their emotions or when they are in a negative cycle with us. When these things happen, our most trusted people can quickly become unsafe until they manage their own emotional state. We should never share from a place of vulnerability with someone who is actively stuck in a reactive and defensive place. We simply should not expect anything good to come out of it.

When evaluating for emotional safety, we can decide our approach to addressing the conflict. When someone is safe, it allows us to enter into a deeper vulnerability in how we approach conflict. In this case, we want to tune into our primary emotion and share it, knowing we will not just address the conflict but have an opportunity for a significant connection to help build a secure attachment. We do not want to attempt this vulnerability if the person cannot respect our vulnerability and perspective.

If we deem someone to be unsafe, we need to take a more surface-level approach to check our understanding of the experience while using curiosity and openness. We will learn more about these approaches later. What is important now is to understand that both approaches rely on us not interpreting or judging others' thoughts or feelings.

We check for safety because it protects us from people who are generally unsafe, or even just unsafe in the moment. It also protects us from being triggered by people who could possibly lead us into greater conflict when we choose the wrong time or approach to address conflict. Finally, the safety check will provide us with the best chance of having a good outcome.

SELF-REGULATION: THE KEY TO UNLOCK THE PRISON

Our emotions do not come out of nowhere. When a person says something hurtful or mean to us, we may react by feeling angry and defensive. Because emotions are so strongly tied to our reactions, it is easy for our emotional experience to live in reactive emotional places. Instead of tuning into our fear or sadness about something hurtful that someone said, we often quickly tune into our reactive emotion of anger or frustration to defend ourselves. These responses leave us stuck in these emotions, which is dysregulating, meaning it leaves us struggling to manage our emotional response and ability to navigate relationships.

If we learn how to self-regulate our emotions, we can avoid the reactive emotional prison we easily create for ourselves. When we get stuck in our own emotional reactiveness, we are left to suffer from the negative interpretations our reactions create within us.

We can see one example of how we create this kind of prison for ourselves by revisiting Mike and another of his dating efforts in which he reacts negatively when the person does not respond to his phone call quickly. In the absence of clear information, he ends up creating his own meaning to explain why they did not call. This meaning-making leads him to be stuck in reactive emotions, and he makes up stories about what the other person is thinking or feeling about him. This process quickly moves from the *fact* of them not calling to an escalation created out of his negative reactions and *interpretations* about why they did not call. He creates more negative interpretations in an endless loop until the person finally calls and apologizes for falling asleep and not calling him. Like Mike, we often put ourselves through much unnecessary turmoil. It can feel like being trapped in a whirlwind of negative thoughts, which does nothing but harm us and often the relationship.

Through self-regulation, we can develop a way to break free from the bondage we have experienced. This is about developing both an *inner* freedom so that we no longer are tortured by our own interpretation and a *relational* freedom when we no longer let our reactive emotional experience dominate how we see our world and others. We can learn to live in a space where we do not react to people's actions as if we know what they think or feel.

Self-regulation is a process of managing our own emotional responses to our world. We do this first by checking our beliefs. It can be challenging for us to realize just how our beliefs influence how we feel about our experiences. Checking our beliefs is an ongoing process of discovery about what we believe, how these beliefs impact us, and if this is what we really want to believe in the first place.

Let's consider the case of how Amy views anxiety. If she believes that anxiety is bad because it means she is mentally ill—and all her negative understandings of what that means—then when she experiences anxiety, she does not just end up with the discomfort of the anxiety itself. She also suffers because of how much more it means to her to have anxiety. However, if she embraces anxiety as a part of her human experience, her understanding of it does not make the experience worse. Instead, it leaves room for her to address what is causing the anxiety in the first place.

In the same way, if we believe we know what another person thinks or feels, like in Mike's situation, we have no choice but to *respond* to our belief. We never engage our curiosity to discover what they actually *do* think. Most of the time, what we believe others are thinking and feeling reflects us being critical of ourselves, and we are left suffering and responding negatively to our own interpretation.

Another part of self-regulation is recognizing and stopping the negative relational cycle as it starts. This cycle leads to both parties becoming more reactive and conflict increasing. When we are able to recognize we are feeling reactive, we can get ourselves away from those we are reacting to and begin working to evaluate our true primary emotion. Getting out of the experience that is triggering us is one of the most self-regulating things we can do.

Moving from reactive emotions to a primary emotion will anchor us in the truth of our experience. An example of this is how when we get angry at someone, it is easy to be stuck in our emotion of anger and not feel like there is an off-ramp. Historically, the only way we resolve anger is if the other person owns *our* interpretations and *our* blame of them, or if it just dissipates over time. Either way, the consequence is disconnection. However, the real off-ramp to our reactive emotions is anchoring ourselves into our primary emotion, which is likely fear. The minute we can tune into the primary emotion of fear, anger is no longer our emotional state.

When it comes to conflict, we don't benefit from arguing our side or what the other person is doing or saying wrong. We need to focus on our own emotional experience. Part of self-regulation is owning that our reactions to others are about something inside us, and the other person is just the object triggering our primary and reactive emotions. It is our responsibility to manage ourselves. Taking responsibility can free us from our own emotional prison, as well as the ability to positively address our conflict with others. In doing so, we build greater connections.

MOVING FORWARD

This chapter has been about the impact and influence of our emotions on conflict. We looked at the dynamics involved with how our experiences are influenced by our reactive emotions, which leads to our meaning-making and the stories that feed the emotional prison we get stuck in. We looked at how the key to leaving our emotional prison is to identify our primary emotion and recognize how this helps to transform our emotional experience. We looked at the importance of checking relationships for safety so we know what approach to conflict might serve us best. We have also seen how self-regulation is essential to changing our reactions to others and our ability to fruitfully address conflict. As we move further, we will take a dive into our view-of-self and the ways this view can influence and motivate us. We will look at how our view-of-self can impact our emotions and our relationships and can often lead to greater conflict with others.

Chapter 5

VIEW-OF-SELF

MIKE CONTINUES TO struggle with his loneliness, questioning his position in life as a single thirty-two-year-old with a limited social life. He had imagined that he would be married with a family at this age, but instead, he lives alone and works long hours. He spends his free time either on dating apps or social media in an effort to connect with others, yet he continues to slip deeper into viewing himself as a failure. He experiences increased desperation as no meaningful relationships emerge from his effort, but he gets stuck thinking that if he stops, he might miss out on finding "the one." However, spending time on dating apps also increases feelings of being unwanted and unloved due to the amount of rejection he experiences. Furthermore, whenever he spends time on social media, searching for connections with friends and family, he winds up with a heightened sense of anxiety and an increasingly negative view of himself because he is constantly comparing his life to other people. He is then stuck viewing his life as "outside of the norm" compared to everyone else, and he can't help but feel like something is fundamentally wrong with him.

We all have an idea of who we are based on many things, including having secure attachment or not to others, body image, experiences, messages from caregivers, capabilities, emotions, and desires. We develop our beliefs about ourselves, in part, by how we see ourselves in relation to others. Many times, other people do not clearly express how they feel about us or how they view us. However, we still end up picking up on their body language, their tone, and the things they say. We allow ourselves to be influenced by how we believe they see us. Thus, our beliefs about what others think of us often become the image we adopt about ourselves.

Our self-image can be positive or negative, and likely is a bit of both. The importance of understanding our image of ourselves is that this becomes a significant part of the filter we use to interpret people and events in our lives. If we are not mindful of the role of our self-image in our interpretation process, we can easily misinterpret others.

In this chapter, we will look at the views we hold about ourselves, explore the importance of belonging, and come to understand factors that shape and negatively impact our view-of-self. We will also see how our view-of-self affects *conflict* and how it can lead to greater escalation. Thankfully, The Confident Communication Model is a tool to help us live a more empowered life as we take ownership of our view-of-self and gain the freedom to live with a greater sense of belonging. We will learn more about The Confident Communication Model later on and how to apply it to our everyday lives.

NEGATIVE SELF-IMAGE

Many of us have a significant negative self-image, whether we recognize it or not, and we have likely developed it in response to the difficulties and challenges we have faced. Unfortunately, our negative view can lead us to struggle with our self-esteem and trusting others. This view often starts with how those who cared for us during our early development communicated messages about us. We made meaning about who we are based on these messages. It is easy to take on a negative self-image when we feel criticized or neglected by others, especially when we are directly told that we are a problem. Consequently, we end up interpreting what others say to align with these views of being faulty or broken, even when that is not what they are saying.

The greatest factor in developing our negative self-image is how we view ourselves, what others think or feel, and our place in society. Often, without even recognizing it, these beliefs impact how we feel, how we interpret our world, and what we think is true. Because of this, it is essential to question *what* we choose to believe and *why*. If we believe that people are untrustworthy because of previous injuries, then we may always struggle to trust others. We will likely take a defensive stance that doesn't allow us to risk intimacy and trust. An alternative approach might be to believe that we *can* trust someone, but first, we should make sure they are emotionally safe for us. We do not need to blindly trust—we can use caution while also believing that people can be trustworthy. By acting this way, we can open the door of opportunity for significant connections and intimacy.

Another belief that develops in response to previous negative experiences is how we perceive limitations to our abilities. For example, Mike had a negative experience in the third grade when presenting a book report that led him to feel humiliated and ashamed in front of his peers. This experience developed into a life-long belief that he could not speak in front of crowds. This shame has led him to avoid presenting or even speaking in front of a crowd; in any situation where he is required to speak in front of people, he experiences extreme anxiety. Mike's belief about his inability to get in front of people has left him with a negative self-image, believing he is the only one who cannot comfortably speak in public. It is not until we begin to understand our beliefs and challenge them that we can begin to live the life we choose instead of one defined by our fears.

Our negative self-image does not end with what we believe about our place in the world; it extends to our inner world and our relationship with ourselves. It impacts how we view our own emotional experiences and leads us to question whether it is okay to feel what we do. Our negative self-image might lead us to take on the role of peacemaker in our relationships, viewing our wants and needs as less important than others' and, instead, focusing on making everyone else happy. In a similar way, if we take ownership of others' emotionally abusive messages about our lack of worth, we will likely believe that we deserve to suffer the way we do.

These messages can keep us from choosing to live a better life. We might settle for abuse out of the belief that we do not deserve to be treated better. We end up handing over our agency to our negative beliefs and those who mirror them back to us. Giving away our agency will cause us greater internal conflict and never lead to the connection and happiness we desire.

A negative self-image can taint the lens through which we make meaning of our experiences. In fact, it can do great harm to our relationships and lead to escalating conflict. The harm comes from interpreting others' words and actions through a lens that is coated in our negative self-image. In these moments, we react, often aggressively, to feeling criticized; but the criticism we experience comes from our negative interpretation of what others meant by their words or actions. A negative self-image will lead to more conflict if we continue to give power to our interpretation instead of dealing with *why* we are interpreting things through this negative filter in the first place.

If our self-image is negative, we can end up feeling disconnected, as if we do not belong or matter—even if we have meaningful, supportive relationships with people in our lives. We can feel broken and believe that everyone else "has it together" and that we are the only ones who do not seem to know how to do this thing called life. However, in my experience as a counselor and coach, many people think they are broken and that everyone else has it together. It is a common experience that people have and just do not share with one another.

Understanding our self-image is so important because it impacts how we experience conflict. We need to recognize what we have believed about ourselves up until now and begin to take ownership of this aspect of our lives. This change will come as we choose to evaluate what we have believed about ourselves, question those beliefs, and decide if that is really what we want to believe. Through this process of mindfulness and empowerment, we choose what we want to believe about ourselves, who we really are, and who we are working to become.

WE ALL WANT TO BELONG

A significant factor impacting our view-of-self is our sense of belonging. How we experience belonging in relationships is core to our survival but also to our ability to thrive. Of course, we prioritize relationships with family, friends, and co-workers, but many relationships also happen through the greater interconnected web of society.

In fact, part of our experience of belonging is our shared dependency on others. Some of these relationships provide services at the center of our daily life, like postal workers, electricians, garbage collectors, and other municipal or state-run service providers. We are also dependent on our medical providers, public transit drivers, and the mechanics who keep our cars working. As you can see, we have a massive web of interconnected relationships, both direct and indirect, that we need in order to live the life we desire.

The greater web of relationships we belong to offers power and opportunity; without these relationships, we would spend all our time in a subsistence lifestyle, focusing on survival and meeting our basic needs for food and shelter. In this same way, we experience interconnected belonging through our contributions in work and social settings and our relationships with others. In the context of our daily lives, belonging is a significant need for our survival that allows for leisure and free time and the space to advance ourselves and our world.

We are part of the greater system of society, and this form of belonging is crucial for our advancement as a species; however, these forms of belonging can be impersonal and not offer a deeper emotional level comparable to the meaningful relationships we aspire to have. Our emotional needs for safety, security, and love can only be met through personal relationships. Furthermore, our individual development and mental and emotional health are significantly impacted, and even formed, by how we belong to these types of communities. This kind of belonging includes family, friends, social groups, co-workers, religious communities, classmates, or a partner. These relationships are the ones in which we develop meaningful emotional attachment and find value by identifying as part of them. In so doing, we develop a more positive self-image.

We all want to belong. We desire meaningful connections with others that nurture our emotional needs. As mentioned earlier, we are not alone in our desire to belong. Yet, we often feel like no one else experiences what we do; we look around and think that everyone easily fits in. When we see others who belong, it often triggers our own longing for deep connection and our desire to matter to others. When we belong, it makes us feel special and gives us the confidence that we matter in a unique way to others. Belonging is relevant because of how foundational relationships are to our life experience. Our feelings of belonging (or a lack of belonging) in relationships have a considerable impact on our quality of life and view-of-self.

IT'S NOT UP TO THEM

Mike grew up in a large family as the third child of five. His parents were not wealthy, and both his mother and father had to work hard to provide the basic necessities. Though his parents greatly valued family, they were often gone and unable to provide individual attention to each kid, which left Mike feeling unseen. His family also had a culture of using harsh sarcasm as a way of relating, which made Mike feel picked on by others. Growing up, Mike seemed to have stronger emotions than his siblings and was more deeply impacted by situations or words. Mike always felt "different," as it seemed like the rest of his brothers and sisters fit easily into his family. His experience of feeling like an outsider impacted his self-image, causing him to believe he did not belong.

Belonging influences how we develop our sense of attachment from our earliest days. If we feel like we belong and are supported by our caregivers early on, we develop a stronger sense of identity and security in relationships; this can set us up to have an easier time feeling a sense of belonging in other relationships as we mature into adulthood. Our childhood has a significant impact on how we feel about belonging and our *ability* to belong.

If our parents died, could not take care of us, or were just unable to provide a safe environment, we may struggle to feel like we belong in other settings as we mature. However, as we see with the example of Mike, we can be loved, have many of our needs met, and belong to a big family, yet still feel like outsiders. Why? Well, if our emotional needs are neglected, it can leave us feeling like we do not belong. When we do not have a deep sense of belonging to the groups we are part of, such as family, friends, or a faith community, we may blame ourselves and struggle to force ourselves to fit in. In reality, we might not feel safe or connected enough with them to feel accepted for who we are. This can make it difficult to feel like we belong—even to groups that we are clearly members of.

When we do not feel like we belong emotionally, we often feel isolated and alone, which can lead to anxiety, depression, and other mental health issues. When this happens, it becomes challenging to risk vulnerability in finding others with whom we can genuinely belong. Our fear of rejection can lead us to reason that if we do not take the risk, then we cannot be rejected. In our attempt to avoid risk, we also remove the possibility of creating connections. We also limit our opportunities to belong. Though caution might make us wait for people to welcome us into their community or relationships, this approach will inevitably result in a lack of connection, and we will blame everyone but ourselves for our failure to connect. But the responsibility of finding places to belong is our own. We need to develop our own agency and recognize our sphere of control over how, and to whom, we want to belong.

Relationships and a sense of belonging are part of everyone's needs; these needs just look different depending on the person. There is not just one way to experience belonging. For example, one of the challenges in achieving our sense of belonging may come from whether we are introverts or extroverts. Introverts focus their energy inwardly and are introspective and enjoy time alone, while extroverts focus their energy outwardly and seek out social interaction with others. While an extrovert may want to be a part of a large and active social group, an introvert may want to be a part of a smaller group of people that does not require that level of active engagement. While introverts like to be alone more than extroverts, this does not mean they want to live in complete isolation. It can be enough for some people to have a small group of close friends to meet their need for belonging; for others, it may require being a part of a large group of friends or a community.

Another challenge in our quest to belong is in our beliefs about what belonging should look like or how it should happen. This can be seen in Mike's experience of moving from Austin to Seattle for his job without knowing anyone. His first year in Seattle was challenging, and he had a difficult time making friends and developing a social life. Mike had grown up in Texas and went to college in Austin, where he had developed a large social network. He had also left a place where the people were incredibly friendly, according to his view. As this was also where he had a strong and supportive friend group, he felt like he belonged there.

During his first year in Seattle, he was incredibly lonely. His way of making sense of how hard it was for him to find community was to adopt a perspective that embraced what people call "The Seattle Freeze." This is the idea that Seattle is unfriendly and cold to newcomers, and people get frozen out from social connections. This made sense to him because he was comparing his feelings of being lonely in Seattle to his feelings of belonging in Austin.

There are several problems with Mike's mean-ing-making. The idea of "The Seattle Freeze" could be a good excuse for why he had such a difficult time finding a community or relationships like what he had in Austin. However, the reality was that he had built his Austin relationships over a long period of time—and at a college. In that setting, it had been easy to interact with a wide variety of people and have the energy and time to build relationships with others who were focused on the same things. It is a massively different experience to move across the country with no connections and try to build friendships as an adult in the professional world.

The term "The _____ Freeze" is used by people to explain experiences in cities around the world. When we move to a new city where we hardly know anyone, we tend to judge our experience of not connecting or finding a place to belong by blaming something besides ourselves. We do this to make sense of our experience, and, in doing so, we label and blame the community as cold because we have not found our way to belong in it. This form of blaming takes away our responsibility for our sense of belonging and puts the responsibility on others. If it is someone else's fault that I am lonely, I have no responsibility for it. Therefore, I don't have to do anything to actively change my circumstance.

Individualistic societies don't put much, if any, emphasis on the importance of community, vulnerability, or relationships. The impact of this is that many of us lack a sense of belonging in our society or even in our own families. When we find even a couple of friends who welcome and embrace us, it is like getting a drink of water in the hottest desert. Our lack of belonging often results from who we are and how we interpret others. If we are closed off, people will probably not warm up to us. If we negatively interpret people's words and actions and live reactive lives by lashing out toward others, we isolate ourselves due to our own thoughts and behaviors.

Our efforts to belong fall squarely on our own shoulders. This is not to say that others do not have a role to play in accepting us; I merely want to emphasize that we will never find a place to be accepted without making an effort to belong. And this effort starts with a positive view-of-self: one that is honest about who we are and what we need.

WE ALL WANT TO MATTER

Belonging and taking part in deep, intimate relationships includes a desire to matter to other people (and that they matter to us as well). In fact, belonging is a core component of feeling like we matter. Mattering to others impacts how we view ourselves, and it influences our understanding of our value and self-worth. I define mattering to others as our belief that others value us, which can serve as an affirmation that we are not as broken and alone as we often feel.

Our desire to matter comes from a drive to be significant and important to others. People who focus on their connection to nature still want to matter as a part of nature. Even people who are not seeking earthly connection still desire to matter to others. People often develop religious beliefs as a part of how they understand themselves and express their desire to matter as part of a greater design. It is healthy to want to matter in any of these ways, but it is important that we understand how these beliefs inform our perspective. Our desire to matter can be a problem if it leads to such rigid views that it ends up harming our self-image and relationships.

We all desperately want to be loved, and even more so by those that *we* love deeply. Being in any meaningful relationship is about loving and caring for one another on the deepest level possible. In this, parents want to matter to their children just as much as children want to matter to their parents. Uncles and aunts want to matter to their nieces and nephews. Siblings want to matter to each other, and friends want to matter to their friends. Most of us end up longing for a partner we can have a unique relationship with, and, in return, we want to know we matter to them in a way no one else does.

As we look back at Mike's experience when he struggled with not getting a quick response from the woman he had just started dating, we see how his past relational injuries haunt him and add to the story that he does not matter. Mike has struggled with feeling like he does not matter to others since he was young, and he did not feel like he belonged in his own family. More recently, he thinks he doesn't matter because he is thirty-two years old, and no one has wanted to be in a relationship with him for longer than nine months. All his relationships have ended with the other person breaking up with him, and he feels incredibly lonely. Mike has made meaning out of his life experiences and created a story about not mattering to others. He has unconsciously chosen to believe this as his truth, and he has taken it on as a central view of himself.

He wants to matter deeply to others but acts out of his negative view of himself, which leads him to react to others from a very defensive place. When he interacts with a potential partner, and something happens that he doesn't understand, he is quick to see it through his negative interpretive lens of not mattering, thus creating a negative reasoning for what must be happening. When the woman he was seeing didn't respond to him quickly, he got stuck in his internal process, creating more negative interpretations on an endless loop. This internal process escalated his anxiety and left him feeling overwhelmed with a flood of negative thoughts. In response, he ended up blowing up her phone with text messages after just a few hours until she finally called and apologized for falling asleep and not calling him back. The disjointed reaction the woman experienced pushed her away and led to the end of their relationship. The breakup reaffirmed his negative interpretation that he does not matter; however, in reality, she liked him but did not like his reactions and behaviors to a small incident in their relationship.

We can easily believe that we don't matter to others. This can happen because of painful life experiences, broken relationships, and relational injuries, just to name a few. When this happens, it can lead us to believe that if we really mattered to others, they wouldn't have treated us the way they did. Our beliefs have a profound impact on how we understand the ways in which we do–or don't–matter to others. If we believe that we do not matter to anyone, we will interpret their expressions of care, support, and love through a lens of doubt and disbelief. We can matter to others and still feel and believe that we do not. The real issue here is that our feelings regarding how we matter are defined by our *own* beliefs about what someone is thinking or feeling about us; they are not defined by the other person's *actual* feelings. How we view ourselves, our attitudes, our self-esteem, and our own mental health are defined by what we believe about ourselves.

If we feel in our minds that we don't matter to others, it can lead us to be defensive and reject even wanting to matter to others. This position does not allow us to entertain the idea that we *want* to matter. If we do not care that we matter, then we cannot experience pain if we end up feeling rejected. This position can also lead us to seek to have our needs met in ways that do not rely on the people that matter to us, such as drugs or alcohol; we might also seek out relationships that temporarily make us feel good but do not give us the deep connection we really desire—deep relationships come from mattering.

When we feel like we do not matter to others, we can end up working even harder to prove that we *do* matter. We can overcompensate by making a lot of money or getting into a position of power whereby the simple nature of our role puts us in a position of mattering, at least to our employer and subordinates. We can become people pleasers in an effort to be accepted and appreciated so that we can get a sense of being wanted. We can decide to have children so that we will have someone to unconditionally love us, at least for a time, because of the nature of their dependence on us. The problem with these approaches is that they all will eventually fall flat if we never develop the ability to feel we matter to others for who we are.

Whether we recognize it or not, our beliefs have a massive impact on our interpretation of others and, ultimately, how we feel about our own place in the world. If we believe that how we feel, think, or act is wrong, then we can easily take on the belief that we are fundamentally wrong. Learning to see and believe in the ways we do matter to others can often lead us to matter to them even more. If we believe we matter to others, we can feel safely vulnerable and learn to share our primary emotions; in doing so, we can build stronger attachment within our relationships.

Our experience of mattering is something that we can cultivate as we learn to develop ourselves and how we live in relationship with others. We can do this by recognizing our beliefs about our world and challenging them, by working to stop interpreting what others are thinking and feeling, and by learning to address conflict in a meaningful way that can improve our connections with others rather than cause greater disconnection.

THE COMPARISON GAME

There is a game that we end up playing without even realizing or choosing to. I will call this "the comparison game." The comparison game is not new; it has historically gone by the name "keeping up with the Joneses." In this game, we compare our lives to what we perceive as the better life that our neighbor is living. In the comparison game, we look at everyone else's lives and judge them based on extremely limited information. This comparison usually leaves us feeling horrible because the parts of others' lives we see from the outside make it seem like everyone else has life figured out and are on track in a way that we are not. We then feel like we are lacking or wrong for how our life is going or how behind we are compared to others. We don't even recognize we are playing the comparison game; we just feel really bad about our own lives, our relationships, our jobs, and so much more.

In the past, this game was limited to the interactions we had with our immediate community. If we had no real relationship with a neighbor, we might compare the things they have, like a car, and make comparisons to our own possessions. With people we were closer to, we might have seen them interacting with their partner at an event and compared our perception of their relationship and family to how we experienced our own relationships and family.

Today, we are playing the advanced version of the game because of our access to information and others on the internet. The game is being played on social media, as we are inundated with images of acquaintances, friends, and even strangers portrayed as living their best lives. Social media plays a dangerous role in our struggle with self-worth because everyone shares the best and happiest images of themselves. It is impossible to spend any time looking at others' images without having some thought flitter through our minds questioning how we are doing in life.

Usually, we are unaware of how we are being impacted by the comparisons we make with others, but we often still end up feeling bad about ourselves and the life we are living. This is not because what we see is true; it is because of how we interpret the images and our belief that they feel happier than we do. However, we do not actually know how others think or feel about their own lives.

Others may be experiencing us the same way, especially if we also only put our best images on social media. This can cause others to think, feel, and believe that our life is much better than their own. Everyone pays the price for playing this game, and that price is increased insecurity, decreased self-worth, and a whole lotta doubt. It has a massive impact on our view of ourselves and our emotional experience. Most of the time, we do not even recognize that we are playing this game.

Unfortunately, there are no winners in the comparison game.

We are all at various stages of life and in our processes of personal growth. These interpretations of others' positions in life are false and do not accurately represent the inner struggles that everyone experiences. Unfortunately, others are looking at the wonderful images we post and are also feeling inadequate. The comparison game does not lead to a life of peace and contentment. Instead, this game continually feeds on our anxiety and fear, which will leave us with a negative view of ourselves, as well as emotional pain and complete dissatisfaction.

In our efforts to respond to these feelings of inadequacy or unhappiness, we will react by doing things to try to live the life we believe we *should* live in an effort to feel happy. The question is: Are we really unhappy because of how our life is? Or because of how we feel when comparing it to how much happier others *seem* to be? This can lead us to believe that we feel the way we do because we have chosen wrong. Maybe we think we chose the wrong partner, job, school, or career, and if we could find the right "whatever," we would be as happy as those we compare our lives to. These feelings can lead us to what has historically been called a "mid-life crisis." But, in today's culture, it is really a "life crisis" because this can happen at any age.

We have the ability to choose how we view ourselves. We may not start from a place of choice, initially just responding to our understanding of how others see us, but we can develop our ability to claim ownership over our self-image. When we are young, our image of ourselves is shaped by the things around us, from the impacts of our parents' or friends' messages, to how society, on a subconscious level, can lead us to adopt a certain image of how we fit into our world. It can be easy for us not to move past defining ourselves through how we are seen or perceived by others, but this will leave us with a self-image that is not of our own choosing, but rather, it's an image that is critical and self-defeating. The more we compare ourselves to others, the more we will harm ourselves.

By recognizing how the game is played, we can choose to *stop* playing the game. We can work toward seeing our world through a clearer lens that determines our success. We do not need to play a game that makes it feel impossible to be happy. Through our own conscious decisions about what we choose to believe and how we choose to see our world, we can find peace as we define our own success.

EMPOWERED FOR CONFLICT

In this chapter, we looked at the impact of our view about ourselves on how we experience and react to conflict in our lives. We explored our desires to belong and be part of something bigger and to matter to others so we can view ourselves in a more positive and meaningful light, instead of the negative views that so easily develop in our subconscious. We also learned how important it is to understand our view-of-self and take ownership of it, leading to our empowerment as we redefine how we see ourselves. We talked about how our negative self-image taints relationships and impacts how we react and are perceived by others in a self-fulfilling and negative way. We also explored how we can be seriously impacted by the comparison game and how, in recognizing that we are playing the game, we can be empowered to stop playing and work to develop a different view of ourselves.

As we have explored our view-of-self, it has opened the door to see how much meaning we make based on other people's thoughts and feelings. In so doing, we create stories about them that lead to greater conflict and can end up reinforcing our negative self-image. In the next chapter, we will address one of the greatest escalators of conflict, our meaning-making. We will develop a deeper understanding of how we make meaning that leads us to develop negative stories that we believe to be true when they are not.

Chapter 6

THE STORIES WE TELL OURSELVES

IN SEASON TWO, episode two of the TV show *Ted Lasso*, Ted (the soccer coach) meets with former star player Jamie at a pub. Someone takes a picture of them and puts it on social media. The team gets ahold of the picture and shares it with the new star player Sam, who has taken Jamie's position. The team says to Sam, "It looks like Jamie is coming back to Richmond," as if they know, based on a picture, what Ted is doing or thinking. In this case, they believe he is meeting with Jamie to bring him back to the team.

The next day at practice, Sam begins talking back defensively to Ted's coaching and says, "You think you can do better?" Sam's tone and body language make it clear that he is upset with Ted, and Ted has no idea why.

Ted pursues Sam to find out what is going on and asks him, "You got something you want to talk about?"

"No," Sam replies flatly.

Ted presses him, questioning his answer. "It seems like you have something on your mind, like, 'I'm angry about some mysterious thing, so I am gonna do some cussing.'"

Sam comes around to say that he is angry, and he is honestly sorry that he cussed at Ted. "I can't believe you're bringing Jamie back to the team," Sam adds.

"What?" Ted questions.

"I saw the picture of you and him on Twitter," Sam replies, as if this says everything that needs to be said. Sam goes on to express how upset he is at the idea of Ted bringing Jamie back and why it is the wrong decision. "You didn't even talk to us about it," he says, revealing some emotion.

"Honestly, Sam, I didn't think there was anything to talk about. I told Jamie it wasn't going to happen," Ted replies. Upon hearing this, Sam is shocked and immediately begins apologizing, recognizing the awkwardness.

In response, Ted kindly expresses, "It is all right."

This is a great example of how the story we tell ourselves can lead us to behave in a way completely out of line with reality. With very little information and the help of his teammate's interpretation of a picture, Sam owned the story that Ted was bringing Jamie back. The only truth in this scenario was that Ted had a drink with Jamie. Every other aspect of the story as to what Ted was doing was wholly made up in their minds.

Sam did what we all do: He ran with the story inside his head and interpreted it as reality. He had created a clear judgment that Ted was willing to harm the camaraderie of the team for a good player. A beautiful part of this interaction is how Ted does not take the bait and get sucked into a negative cycle. Instead, he keeps himself open to understanding what is going on with Sam by cultivating curiosity and support. He does not simply react to Sam's criticism with his own emotional response of anger or frustration; he expresses understanding and love for him.

We have been creating stories all our lives, which sets us up to have *historical* versions of our stories that feed the creation of today's active stories. Since birth, we have created stories that define our understanding. We have worked hard to make sense of our world and understand it to the best of our ability. We take in information, interpret it by making meaning out of it, and create our story in a way that determines what we believe to be our truth. The problem is in how our true perceptions can create false facts. In other words, we can use our true perceptions to create a story that is untrue, though it can still contain some factual truths within it.

In this chapter, we will focus on the ways in which we make meaning and how it leads to owning a story. We will explore the problems with our meaning-making and how it can lead us to believe things that are not actually true without ever realizing it. Then, we will work to develop a new way to see our world and deconstruct our meaning-making so that we can find freedom from the bondage of negative emotions.

MEANING-MAKING: THE NEED FOR SECURITY AND THE DESIRE FOR CONTROL

When in the middle of a complex or perplexing situation, most of us probably don't ask, "What meaning do I make of this?" However, to me, this is surprising, considering that each and every day, we are "meaning-making" almost constantly.

But what is meaning-making? It is the process by which we take in information, interpret it, and create an understanding of it. When we believe we know *why* things happened, it tends to provide us with a feeling of security. We anchor ourselves in our interpretation because it gives us a sense of control over our circumstances. One form of meaning-making is how we work to develop an understanding of circumstances that are outside of our control, often in the wake of larger events or experiences such as a terrorist attack, a loved one's death, or other traumatic life events. Meaning-making stems from our desire to comprehend why things happen. However, too often, we really cannot know the reason.

Another form of meaning-making is a more constant, everyday experience surrounding what other people are thinking and feeling. This form of meaning-making has a massive impact on our emotional well-being and our experience of others, often leading to increased conflict with the people in our lives because we interpret what they mean by their words or actions. We don't conduct this process of meaning-making on a cognitive level. In fact, it happens so automatically and so quickly that we usually do not even recognize it. We often end up feeling and believing that our interpretations of the other's intent, feelings, and thoughts are the truth.

An example of meaning-making can be seen in Mike's recent breakup and his need to make sense of why she was ending their relationship. The breakup happened soon after he had a strong emotional reaction to her not responding to his phone call quickly enough. No matter how many times Mike asked her to explain why she was ending their relationship, her reasoning, "I don't see a future together," was not enough for Mike. He could not make sense of why this was happening.

In breakups, we often don't even get the opportunity to discover the *why* because the end of the relationship ends all communication. Other times, like in Mike's case, we cannot make sense of the other person's choices, so we try again and again to get them to explain it to us. We have hope that, somehow, if we talk about it enough and come to an understanding, we will be okay with why they ended things. In the process, we often end up with an interpretation that allows us to feel better by blaming them, or we feel worse because we blame our own inadequacies for the end of the relationship. In Mike's situation, not knowing why this happened left him adopting a very negative interpretation that reasoned it was because he was unlovable and flawed, and no one would want to be with him.

The exercise of trying to get answers from the other person is a desperate effort to acquire enough information to make meaning out of what happened. The outcome is that we make the best sense we can out of what we know, or think we know, and choose to believe our own interpretation in the same way Mike did.

There are several problems with this approach, the main one being that we still really do not know why it ended. We didn't acquire the "information" we sought. The other person likely could not fully express why they wanted to end the relationship even if they wanted to, or they may not even know what led to the end of the relationship themselves. When this happens, we are left answering the question "Why?" on our own. Any meaning we make about these events is only our best guess and never the truth. The reality is we want to feel the comfort and control that understanding can provide—and this goes for many situations in life, not just breakups. When we are in a position where we do not have a clear understanding, we tend to make our own meaning in an effort to feel comfort and control, and we often do this by abandoning truth.

BREAKING OUT OF THE BOX

As we've already touched on, meaning-making reflects our desire for control in our lives. We do not like the discomfort or fear we experience when we lack control; fear often drives our desire to make meaning because meaning offers a sense of peace. However, the peace we feel is the result of our interpretation and is not rooted in reality. Our desire for control leads us to put our world into a box of our own understanding. We develop ways of defining the world that put it all into a neat little package that makes us feel safe and secure. We will even stretch our reasoning and interpret new information in a way that fits our box instead of allowing it to challenge our framework, which risks sending us into the space of the unknown.

An example of maintaining the boundaries of our box is when we are dogmatic about something like religion. We can know scripture incredibly well and interpret our world through this lens, but at what point does our ability to quote a passage as an answer limit our understanding of God? Are we putting God in a box because we assume we know everything about Him? Or are we living with the mystery of a God that is beyond our understanding?

We can put our world in a box by seeing everything through a lens that takes in information and interprets what people think or feel. If we believe our interpretations of the world are factual, our belief system has no space for others' experiences, feelings, interpretations, or understandings. If anyone sees things differently, we are left believing they are lying to us, gaslighting us, or just plain wrong.

The space of the unknown is often the truth of our lives, rather than the fixed interpretations we assign. The world has far more mystery and unanswerable questions than we are comfortable with, which requires us to accept and live in the tension of having many questions with few answers.

My hope for all of us is that the unknown does not keep us from asking questions but instead helps us to live in a constant state of curiosity, asking more questions without *needing* to know the answer. Our challenge is to learn to be content with the unknown and enjoy the exploration of life's mysteries. If we can embrace living in the tension of not knowing, it can provide us with the mental and emotional freedom we are seeking.

ACCEPTING THE PARADOX

Another challenge in our process of meaning-making is how we interpret things in terms of dichotomies, or the idea that there are two mutually exclusive ways of seeing something and only one is right. So much of the world does not exist in black or white, nor does it exist in shades of gray. We live in a place of paradox, where multiple things are true at the same time about the same thing. Accepting this paradox is hard for us, as we have been trained to see things as black and white, good and evil, right and wrong. We end up in situations where we feel like we are forcing our understanding of something to fit into one of two sides. We often end up defaulting to the most dominant position as the "truth" and dismissing the other one. If our emotions contradict our beliefs about what is true, we sense our own feelings are wrong, which often requires us to dismiss them altogether.

An example of this paradox can be seen when we look back at Sara's story of discovering that her previous therapist—someone who had helped her so much in processing her own sexual assault—had just been arrested for sexually assaulting a woman. Her dominant feeling was hatred for what he had done, but the paradoxical reality of her experience was that she was grateful to him for helping her personally in significant and meaningful ways. He held a special place in her heart because of his work to support her. She struggled to make sense of the news about his arrest because she kept trying to reconcile unreconcilable emotions and truths. The only answer to her paradoxical dilemma was to accept that both contradictory positions were true about the same person.

Another example of this can be seen in Ben's experience. Ben's wife died suddenly in a car accident, leaving him a single father with two young kids. Ben and his wife had a tumultuous relationship, and the day she died was the day he was going to tell her that he was leaving her and wanted a divorce. The complexity of his feelings is the same as anyone might feel; he was sad at the death of his wife and that his children had lost their mother, but he was happy to be out of a relationship that he could not tolerate any longer. Both of his emotional experiences were true about the same event for completely different reasons. He struggled to accept feeling relief that the relationship was over, and he did not believe it was okay to feel that way. To Ben, his feelings of relief were the same as saying, "I am happy she's dead," when, in fact, he was merely happy to be out of the relationship. Ben felt free when he was finally able to accept that both emotional experiences and positions were true at the same time about the same situation. He no longer needed to believe that he was wrong for having more feelings about her death than just sadness.

Just like Sara and Ben, we all have experiences regularly that lead us to paradoxical emotions. This is why it is important that we understand what it is that we are doing in our own meaning-making process. When we do not understand our meaning-making, it naturally leads us to develop stories that shape our beliefs; thus, our reactions to our experiences and others are not aligned with truth.

WE DON'T JUST FIND STORIES IN BOOKS

When we interpret and make meaning out of the events in our lives, as well as others' thoughts and feelings, we create stories. A story, in this context, is our created understanding of a situation or the thoughts and feelings of others composed into a narrative. Our stories feel true and can quickly move from our interpretation to our beliefs—with little to no effort. The problem with this is that while our stories may have factual insights and understanding, the overall meaning we make is not based on the truth.

One example of creating a story can be seen in Scott's reaction to Julie. Julie had just come home from work and greeted Scott. After a few minutes, she asks him, "Did you walk the dog?"

He immediately lashes out at Julie in response to the story he created about her that says, "She doesn't believe that you are able to take care of even the simplest task of walking the dog."

"You don't trust that I can take care of anything. I'm a grown man, Julie! What the hell?" he yells, causing a fight that escalates and lasts for hours.

In this example, Scott has created his own understanding of what Julie is thinking, when in reality, the only fact is that she asked him the question, "Did you walk the dog?" Scott created a story in response to his own history: growing up the youngest of three brothers in a home where he had felt constantly disregarded and labeled as irresponsible. This, along with his strong interpretive lens, left him unable to recognize the meaning-making he was doing.

Our meaning-making is impacted by the interplay between reactive and primary emotions. Our stories develop out of a place of reaction, and the reactive emotions that follow end up defining what has happened. The main problem with stories is that we often do not even recognize we are creating them. Instead, we tend to define our stories as our understanding of a situation or even just the truth about a situation.

Our stories become powerful and feel so true because of the feedback loop between the meaning we make and the emotions that are evoked in response to it. In other words, we receive information, we make meaning about this information, and then we have an emotional response to the meaning we have made. Our emotional responses, in turn, reaffirm that our original meaning-making was accurate, which leads us to believe that the story we created is the truth. In a fraction of a second, we turn our emotional response into a "common sense" understanding that we have never questioned.

Our stories define how we view relationships with our children, parents, siblings, in-laws, coworkers, managers, employees, and partners. Once we have created a story about someone, we are quick to make meaning of the current situation based on the historical story we already have. The historical story plays a significant role in feeding our emotional interpretation of the present story. In this process, the historical story strengthens the "truth" of our original interpretation. We experience this often in the workplace because of the professional and impersonal nature of our relationships and the focus on tasks over relationships. The environment itself is set up to be fertile ground to grow stories.

Coming back to Scott's example, in addition to his stories about his relationship, he also creates stories about his job. He works at a local tech company and has intensely high demands on him, as does everyone he works with. Meetings are constant throughout the day in fifteen-minute increments, leaving little time to get his work done or to answer the hundreds of emails he receives each day. He expresses to his manager his anxiety and stress and that he always feels like a failure because of the overwhelming demands he experiences. His manager sympathizes with him, acknowledges his experience, and expresses that he also feels this way. This leaves Scott feeling heard, supported, and even hopeful for a while.

After a few weeks, when nothing has changed, Scott talks to his manager again to communicate his frustrations.

Again, he is supported, but there is no tangible change. Scott then creates a story about the company and his manager that says, "We are all just cogs in their machine, and they don't care about us." From this point forward, every time something happens at work that he is unhappy about, he draws on this historical story. This story ends up having a toxic impact on his own mindset and attitude and leads him to spread this toxicity to his coworkers as he shares his story with them.

The reality is that Scott does not know how the company and leadership view him or the other employees. However, what *is* true is the negative impact his story has. Scott's story about his company leaves him feeling isolated, defeated, and stuck in his emotions of frustration and anger.

Often with our negative stories, we look to share them with others for affirmation about our experiences. When others buy into our story, it sets up another person to buy into our negative interpretation, who now owns it as their story too. We end up causing them harm as the negative story has an impact on their moods, attitudes, and quality of life. When we do this, we prove true the adage "misery loves company." This highlights the importance of developing a clear awareness of our current and historical stories so that we do not cause ourselves or others unnecessary harm.

In the same way that we impact others when we share our negative stories, we need to understand how we can also be significantly impacted when others share their negative stories with us. When we accept and take on someone else's negative story, we allow it to have power in our lives. Whether it originated from us or someone else, once we accept a negative story as truth, its impact on our lives is huge.

As we look back at Scott's reaction to Julie's question, "Did you walk the dog?" we see him react by lashing out angrily at Julie. Julie then struggled to make sense of Scott's response. She immediately reacted to his critical and judgmental response by angrily yelling back at him in defense. Julie was stuck trying to defend herself and get Scott to see that his interpretation of what she did was incorrect. However, all Scott could see was how defensive and angry she was at him. As a result, *he* was unable to hear what she was really trying to communicate. No matter how hard Julie worked to get Scott to see that his interpretation was wrong, Scott could not hear that his interpretation was wrong. They continued in a negative cycle for hours, reacting to each other's reactions.

One of the greatest challenges we face in relationships is how we experience others' stories about us. When others interpret our thoughts and feelings according to their own story, their interpretation will be true to them; usually, nothing we do or say can convince them otherwise. When we work to defend ourselves against another person's story, they will often take the position of saying that we are either lying or trying to gaslight them. This is an

incredibly stuck place to be in that causes us to feel powerless as our perspective and reality are completely rejected.

When someone else has a story about us that they
rigidly hold onto, our only recourse is to evaluate if their
position or rigidity is because of how they see their world
or is in reaction to being in a negative cycle with us. If it
is related to a negative cycle, then once the cycle is gone
and the strong reactive emotions have subsided, their
defensive position will falter. If, on the other hand, it is
due to a lens that cannot accept others' perspectives, we
will be left with the tension of their interpretation of us.
Often, nothing we do can help them see our perspective,
no matter how hard we try.

The hardest part of learning to manage our stories
is learning to live in the tension that comes with thinking our story might be true but honestly not allowing
ourselves to take a position either way. Too often, we
end up holding onto our story in place of living in this
tension of the unknown. We do not like to live in this
uncomfortable space, but it is necessary if we want to stay
grounded in our truth.

REALITY VERSUS INTERPRETATION

Our stories lie to us! It is important that we begin to differentiate our stories from reality because the stories we
create and own without verifying become like cancerous
tumors in our hearts. We often approach our stories from

a position of thinking we *know* why things happen; we *know* why people did what they did; we *know* what others are thinking or feeling. The truth is, *we do not know!*

We need to develop our ability to recognize when our own stories and those belonging to others are active. If we are having an emotional reaction to someone, it is likely that we have created a story that we are reacting to. In this same way, we can recognize others' stories by picking up on how they are reacting through their body language, tone, or even a shift of the energy in the room.

Our work is to fight the lies of our story and to differentiate fact from our own creation. We can differentiate what is true by simply asking questions and evaluating: What are the observable facts about the situation? And what meaning am I making out of it? This simple step helps us to move outside of our emotional response to our story and start to acknowledge and own the meaning-making involved in creating it.

Part of what makes the stories we create feel so true is the emotions they invoke. Because these emotions feel so powerful, our natural tendency is to define our understanding of our story as accurate and true. The negative stories we create do not serve us or benefit our lives. They come out of our fear and insecurities and lead us to positions of aggression and defensiveness in the context of relationships. Our stories are the main factor that leads us into conflict with ourselves and others and have amazing power to escalate and trap us in these conflicts.

Our stories also act as a barrier to meaningful relationships. We all want to belong and matter to others, but our negative stories directly work against this as they lead us to believe the worst of others and how they think of us. This leads us to live a life focused on protecting and defending ourselves. It becomes very hard to trust and believe that others care when our stories interpret their thoughts and actions as something else.

Once we recognize we have created a story, we need to work to understand it. We do this by understanding and separating the observable facts from the story about those facts that we have created. We are working to separate the truth from the lies in our story. When we can recognize that our story is not the truth, we can let go of the emotional hold our story has over us. This can lead us to emotional freedom, as we no longer are in bondage to our created story and the negative emotional experience it immerses us in.

IS THIS FACT?
THE ALL-IMPORTANT QUESTION

As already demonstrated, Scott had a history of quickly reacting to simple things Julie asked or said, interpreting them as a criticism of himself. They did a good deal of work on their relationship, and over time, Scott was able to develop his self-awareness and come to recognize when he was triggered by his own reactive emotions. He then developed his ability to understand what his emotions were speaking to him and recognize the meaning-making and stories he was creating in response. Due to his efforts, he transformed his interactions with Julie. This was demonstrated when Julie asked Scott at a different time, "Did you take the garbage out?"

Her question triggered him like her questions had so many times in the past, but this time, he recognized his reactive emotional experience and excused himself to go and deal with what he was feeling. He gave himself time to de-escalate his reactive emotions, and then he was able to follow them to his primary emotion of fear. He recognized his primary emotion was the fear that Julie thought he was irresponsible. He also recognized that the story that he had created was that "she sees me as irresponsible." He couldn't shake that this might be true, so he went back to Julie and shared.

"I had a strong reaction to your question about taking out the garbage. I realized that I am afraid that you see me as irresponsible and that this has come alive again. Can I check that story with you? Do you see me as irresponsible?" he asked. Scott vulnerably shared his primary fear with her and was not reactive like he had been so many times in the past. He approached the situation not fully believing his story, but from a position that it might possibly be real and he still needed her help to shake it. Because of his approach, Julie was very open and responsive to his needs.

"No, that is absolutely not how I see you. I know you are a very responsible person, and I was just checking to see if we still needed to take out the garbage because pickup day is tomorrow," she replied.

Recognizing and understanding our stories are the first steps in dealing with them. Then we must decide what to do with our stories because they do not just disappear. However, we do not yet have enough information to determine if the story we created by what we factually observed is true. When we do not differentiate story from fact, we are left responding defensively to the "truth" of our created story and our own negative interpretation of others' thoughts and feelings about us.

In our interactions with others, this may require the input of the other person involved to verify whether the story we created and how we interpreted it was accurate or not, just like how we saw Scott do with Julie. There are other times when we can determine that our stories are not true without others' input. In these instances, we can evaluate for ourselves that the story we created came out of our own issues, fears, or insecurities. When we own these realities, it gives us the ability to let go of our story.

MOVING FORWARD

We just explored some of the biggest factors that lead us into conflict with others. We have explored our tendency to make meaning as a way of understanding and having control over our experiences, how our mean-ing-making leads us to interpret others' thoughts and feelings and create stories about what is happening, and how these stories are often not true. We looked at how even though our stories are not always true, we usually never question them but instead take them on as our reality. We have also learned about the dynamics that get us to these negative stories and how they have such a negative impact on our view-of-self as well as how we see others and approach relationships, leading us into constant conflict. This work of addressing the negative stories we tell and coming to know the truth instead of our interpretations is essential.

Now that we better understand the ways we try to have control over our lives by using our interpretations to put our world into a box and limit others and ourselves in a negative way, we will move on to look at the positive ways we can have control over aspects of our lives and produce wonderful outcomes. We will do this by learning how we can live an empowered life. This includes learn-ing that we have the ability to choose our attitudes, we have the power of being a lifetime learner, we have the ability to choose our own story, and we can find freedom in choosing to live in a mindset of "I don't know."

Chapter 7

LIVING AN EMPOWERED LIFE

WE LEARNED EARLIER that Amy's struggle with anxiety stems from her negative story about mental health and her beliefs about anxiety itself. Her anxiety is only worsened by her ongoing desire for control in her life. She has spent her life making meaning out of every circumstance, as if knowing the "why" will provide her with a sense of control.

Amy was previously unable to tolerate not knowing why someone had done or said something hurtful or why certain situations happened to her or the people she loved. She always quickly found an answer or reason for the circumstances according to the story inside her; these "reasons" gave her a false sense of control and comfort. Her interpretations came out of her desire for control instead of a mindful process of understanding and evaluating each situation. Her story often led her into emotional distress as her autopilot thinking left her with negative meaning-making and the negative emotions that accompanied it.

As she grew in her understanding of the relational dynamics that feed conflict, she began to see how her fear of the unknown caused her to seek control over things she could not control. As she grew in her ability to embrace this lack of control, she began to recognize the areas of her life in which she actually *did* have some power. She recognized areas of self-empowerment that could provide a sense of control over her interpretation of the world and how her perspective led to her feelings. In this process, she was able to develop an understanding and control over her own emotional experiences and responses.

We have spent a great deal of time looking at the ways we make meaning out of our experiences and how our desire for control often has negative outcomes because we can't control everything. In this chapter, we will be looking at areas of our life that we *do* have the ability to control and, when we do, can produce amazingly positive outcomes. We will look at areas of personal empowerment we can control, which include: our thinking, our emotional experience, our reactions to others, our attitude and outlook on life, how we approach our interpretive process about the world, how we approach learning, the stories we choose to believe, our approach to conflict with others, and how a mindset of "I don't know" can produce emotional freedom.

This chapter will explore how living an empowered life can transform our outlook and emotional experience in significant ways, allowing us to chart our own course versus living on autopilot. We *can* develop a mindset that gives us power and control over aspects that can produce very positive outcomes, both in our view-of-self and our relationships with others.

HOW DO WE LOOK AT THINGS?

Our quality of life is largely determined by our outlook and attitude. First, we need to learn to manage our stories and meaning-making. For example, if we view the statement "life happens" as a commentary about how we should not hold so tightly to our desire for control, it can help us live better with the tensions of life. However, if we interpret the phrase as "life is just going to happen, and we are powerless to influence it," we are left with an attitude of powerlessness. These contrasting interpretations demonstrate how important it is that we recognize the ways we interpret information. We have a choice—we *can* shape our outlook and attitude in a way that makes life more enjoyable.

In our work of becoming empowered to own our story, we can choose to take the radical step to assume the best of others. For most of us, we easily default to interpreting others' thoughts and feelings with a critical lens that judges them negatively. The idea that we can have an outlook and attitude that assumes the best of others' intentions, thoughts, and feelings is a place of emotional freedom. By choosing this perspective, we can positively shape our emotional experience, attitude, and reactions to others, leaving us feeling better and with the ability to approach relationships from a more positive position.

One component that is important in our mindset is hope. Hope is one of the greatest motivators in helping us achieve our goals. Too often, we confuse hope with expectation, and in so doing, we can end up rejecting hope altogether. Hope is our desire to want something to happen. Having hope can lead us to feelings of expectation, moving us from our *desire* that something will happen to embrace an *expectation* that it will happen. These two positions, though related, are very different and lead to very different emotional experiences.

Hope can be a great tool that keeps us motivated toward a goal if we can hold onto it loosely enough that it doesn't become a need or expectation. When we have hope that someone will like us and want to be in a relationship with us, and it does not happen, we are hurt and disappointed but can move on rather quickly. When our hope that someone will like us turns into an expectation that they *need* to like us, it feels like getting hit with a ton of emotional bricks when they don't. We are devastated.

In contrast, we often respond to experiences in ways that protect us from a perceived emotional danger and lack of control. An example of this perception is tied to the idea that "if we do not hope, we cannot feel the pain of having it dashed." Instead of allowing ourselves to feel the pain that would come from being disappointed, we force ourselves into the emotional suffering of hope-lessness on an ongoing basis long before we know any outcomes. The dysfunctional ways we work to protect ourselves can end up being more harmful than the thing we fear.

Another way this can happen is when we try to control our lives by assuming the worst possible outcomes so that we will not be disheartened by what ends up happening. However, in doing so, we end up living with the negative emotions that come with expecting the worst of everything. Living this way does not make us feel any better, nor does it change the outcome when something bad does happen. Examples of this include applying for a job or going on a first date and automatically assuming we are not going to get the job or that our date did not like us. In our thinking, it is easier to assume the worst rather than lean into what we want or hope.

We choose to live in a negative mindset, with the negative emotions that accompany it, because we believe this mindset will reduce the pain of rejection. The reality is that rejection hurts the same whether we expect it or not. When we have a protective frame of thinking based on choosing to believe the worst about a situation as we wait to learn the actual outcome, we live in the negative mindset we have chosen and allow it to direct our negative emotions and negative reactions.

A negative outlook leads to a negative attitude which, in turn, leads us to experience ourselves and our world negatively. It shapes how we feel about ourselves and our world and can lead to anxiety and depression. If we focus on the negative, the toxicity of how we see our world can color our interpretive lens and lead us to view everything in a cynical way. In the same way, if we choose an attitude of gratitude and actively pursue this outlook, it sets a tone that is upbeat and appreciative of our world. What we choose to focus on determines the outlook that drives our attitude.

An example of how our outlook impacts our attitude can be seen in how we make meaning out of not being in a relationship. We might be quick to blame being alone on other people and things. In these moments of blaming others, we don't recognize how we are showing up—or not. We need to question if we bring an outlook and attitude of openness and friendliness that invites the same in return. We often get back what we give to others, and if our outlook is that people are unfriendly, we will mirror this attitude. If we want to be part of a community, it may require us to take on an attitude of responsibility and work to be a catalyst that brings people together, and not just wait for others to reach out to us.

The work of choice starts with first learning to recognize the stories we are creating, as well as our historical stories, so that we can truly and mindfully evaluate why we have them and if they are really the truth we *want* to believe. This is an active and mindful practice of engaging our inner world and questioning how and why we think what we do and then choosing to take ownership of it. By defining our story, we are empowered to choose it as our truth in moments of conflict.

Until now, the work of addressing our stories has been focused on managing our negative stories and choosing the story and truth we want instead of our autopilot thinking. But what about checking and managing stories that are positive? We manage negative stories because of the negative impact they have on our conflict with ourselves and our relationships with others. The only time we really need to manage our positive stories is if we are using them as a coping mechanism to avoid dealing with hard issues in our lives. We can sometimes create false positive stories that cause us harm and lead us to deny the reality of others' abuse and injuries against us. In this context, they are really negative stories, just wrapped in positivity. We should be on guard against negative stories in any form, even if they seem positive.

We easily get caught up in living a life of reactive emotions based on our negative stories, not facts. I refer to this as living on autopilot, where we constantly define our world based on how we feel in response to an interpretation that we have not mindfully evaluated or chosen. In the next section, we will explore what it means to live on autopilot.

STOP LIVING ON AUTOPILOT

Living on autopilot means that we determine what is true based on our meaning-making about events and interactions without conscious awareness or choice. Autopilot means that we accept our understanding without any mindful recognition of why we think what we do. It is both natural that we do this and immensely harmful. We end up accepting autopilot as our truth.

An example of autopilot thinking and its impact on a couple can be seen in an interaction between Julie and Scott. Toward the end of their weekly date night, during which Scott made a special dinner for Julie, Julie clears the table and puts the dishes in the dishwasher. A little later, Scott goes to add something to the dishwasher and sees that Julie has put their sharp knives in it. He has repeatedly asked Julie not to put the knives in the dishwasher because he believes it damages them. So, he asks her, "Did you realize you put the sharp knives in the dishwasher?"

Julie, who is letting her autopilot thinking dictate her response, gets very upset because she has interpreted his question to be a criticism of her competency and ability to be a responsible adult.

"Why did we even move in together if I can never do anything right for you?" she shoots back, tears welling up in her eyes.

"What are you talking about, Jules? I was just wondering if you recognized that you did it again," Scott replies, genuinely confused.

Julie doesn't realize that Scott's response is genuine and escalates the conflict to the point where she jumps to questioning their future together. Scott responds by trying to counter Julie's story and assures her that he does not see her as always doing things wrong. However, Julie can only hear this as a lie and an effort to gaslight her.

Like Julie's response above, the rigidity created by our autopilot thinking leads us to believe we know what others are thinking and feeling. In this situation, Julie feels like Scott is gaslighting her when it is not how Scott is actually experiencing this conversation. If we allow our autopilot thinking to take control, we may end up flying straight into a mountain. We have the ability to shape the quality of our lives, but it requires us to take ownership of it and make real efforts to change how we think.

I've got good news for you: Getting out of autopilot thinking is one of the ways we can start to live an empowered life. We can become empowered by recognizing and controlling our meaning-making. Examples of self-empowerment are choosing to believe that "we can do hard things" or "we can handle anything that comes our way." Choosing our attitude and outlook is not hard, but it takes real effort to break free from the automatic ways we react to our world. While it is easy to default to our instinctual interpretations, that does not make them true or helpful for how we seek to live our lives.

The work of empowerment starts with recognizing that our automatic way of understanding the world does not lead to truth but instead to a position of interpreting and defending ourselves from perceived threats. If we develop an outlook based on seeing things in a positive light, it impacts our attitude as well as how we approach relationships and conflict.

CHOOSE SELF-EMPOWERMENT: BE A LIFETIME LEARNER

It can be easy to lose motivation for personal development and rely on autopilot thinking when the factors that motivated us in the past are no longer there, and we stop striving to improve ourselves. Or when we get into a position of being overwhelmed by the demands of life and no longer feel like we have the bandwidth to invest in our own growth. We may have a great job and a good income, and the family we always wanted. Maybe we no longer feel any pressure to challenge ourselves. Without these outside forces, we might not recognize what else we could be striving for. It is easy to end up in a position where we do not recognize it is possible or desirable to change. We know we are in this position when we say things like, "This is just who I am" or, "If people don't like who I am, screw them." We allow autopilot thinking to create a default version of ourselves. We choose to fight anybody that challenges us toward change while allowing our automatic reactive emotions and behaviors to control us. If we do not believe we can change, we never will.

What *should* motivate us in life comes from our answer to the question, "*Who* do we want to be?" This is not the same question as "What do we want to do?" or "What do we want out of life?"; it requires us to know who we want to be in terms of our character and our mental and moral qualities. These characteristics are interpersonal and attitudinal, and they make up who we are to ourselves and others. In turn, they end up defining the quality of our life and relationships. We should truly evaluate and choose for ourselves the characteristics we want based on their impact on our life. What we choose to value and focus on as we develop our character determines everything, from how we feel about ourselves to how we approach relationships. Our choices affect how we approach relationships and deal with conflict.

The process of addressing conflict in our lives should lead us to embrace character traits that help us toward this end. In our work of addressing conflict, we need to do more than just gain a couple techniques to fix how we relate to others. We need a more significant process of embracing change within ourselves. We need to ask how embracing character traits can positively impact our lives and help us in the process of addressing conflict within ourselves and with others. Some helpful character traits are curiosity, lovingness, kindness, graciousness, compassion, empathy, hopefulness, patience, understanding, determination, honesty, leadership, trust, and loyalty.

We should be cautious that we do not approach our desire to grow from a negative perspective, focused on ways we feel lacking or do not feel like we're enough for others. Some negative characteristics that might not serve us well are stubbornness, reactiveness, rudeness, egocentrism, greed, arrogance, anger, apathy, harshness, and jealousy.

It is easy to get stuck in a negative feedback loop between what we believe and how we feel. Our ability to choose the stories we live by can change this. Our outlook and attitude establish whether this feedback loop will be positive or negative. If we have a mindset that we need a certain amount of sleep each night and then we do not get that amount, we will feel tired. If we have a mindset that whatever sleep we get will be enough, then we are far more likely to feel satisfied no matter the amount of sleep we get. In this same way, if we believe we are a night person, we are limiting our ability to be anything else. It is not just how we see ourselves; it is the belief that we are this way *at the core*. How could we expect ourselves to change if this is what we believe to be true?

Instead, let's look at growth as the idea of being a lifetime learner and focusing on positive characteristics as a way of setting goals for ourselves that help us become more than we currently are. In the process, we should also accept and appreciate who we are today and our desire to improve and grow in the first place.

Being a lifetime learner is not about working to meet others' expectations of learning. It is about embracing our own process and pace of learning. Becoming a lifetime learner is a simple choice to embrace a vision of continual personal growth. It requires working to become the person we choose to be. We will never arrive at perfection. We will continuously fail and succeed to different degrees, but our efforts toward transformation offer us freedom from the emotional burdens we currently carry.

Furthermore, being a lifetime learner is not just about learning more about ourselves; it's also about learning more about others. This is essential to developing our ability to easily address conflict. Without the belief that we need to learn more, we will not have the curiosity necessary to properly address conflict in our lives. If we think we already know everything, we will be bad at relationships altogether. Accepting what we do *not know* allows us to learn what others think and feel and actually see who they are, not just relying on who we interpret them to be.

CHOOSING "I DON'T KNOW" AS OUR INTERPRETIVE LENS

In relationships, if we have a story that our partner is critical of us and thinks we do everything wrong, we feel insecure and interpret everything they say through the lens of this story, which makes us feel worse with every interaction. We may even start to view them as our enemy. On the other hand, if we believe that our partner cares deeply for us and has a kind heart, we feel secure, even when they say critical words; we rely on the truth of the story we have chosen about their kind heart, and it positively impacts how we feel about the interaction.

Another component of living an empowered life is learning that we have the ability to choose our own mindset. We have control over our thought processes, outlook, and perspective. This empowered control over our thoughts comes out of our emotional intelligence, mindfulness, and the choices we make in response to the way we perceive our world. If we look back at Julie's response to Scott asking her if she recognized she put sharp knives in the dishwasher, we can see how there could have been a different outcome if Julie had adjusted her mindset to one that "didn't know" and questioned his intent and sought clarity by asking, "Why are you asking me this?" or "Are you criticizing me?" In asking these questions, she might have ended up with a different belief based on his clarification of the situation.

This could have provided her with a different emotional experience, as well as avoiding a fight.

When it comes to conflict, we can get stuck in a web of expectations and interpretations. Our interpretation and the story we create about what someone has done affects our expectation of that person. These expectations, in turn, have an emotional impact on our inner world. The expectations we have and the way they are created by our story reveal the truth we believe. We think we know what others are thinking and feeling to the point that our expectations of them are absolute fact, and when they do not meet these expectations, they can fail us in major ways. This has a significant impact on how we view them as well as how we can end up approaching them in relationships with aggression in reaction to them failing our expectations.

The reality is that we do not know what other people are thinking or feeling, but we think we do. However, there is no greater freedom than our ability to embrace the phrase "I don't know." This phrase is our key to freedom in our mindsets and should constantly be on the tip of our tongue. We gain this freedom by allowing ourselves to accept that we do not know what people mean, what they are thinking, or how they feel unless they explicitly tell us. When we believe we know what others think or feel, we interpret what they say or do and create stories about them. Once we own a story that we have created, we are emotionally bound to it and all its negative interpretations.

If we own a position of "I don't know" instead, it allows us to hold our interpretive story as a possibility, not a fact. When we do not know, we can stay in a position of emotional neutrality. This allows us to address issues and leave room to check our story without the emotions that would have been present if we believed our story was the truth.

An example of this can be seen as we revisit an experience Brian and Sara had when they first started dating. Brian and Sara met on a dating app and were clear in their initial interactions that both had a desire for a serious relationship. One night, after they had been dating for six months, they got into a discussion about their relationship.

"We're not going out," Sara said casually, mid-conversation.

Brian didn't know how to respond—he thought they were on the same page. "Have you been dating other people still?" he asked.

"Yes," she replied matter-of-factly.

Upon hearing this, Brian shut down and ended the conversation. Soon after, he left her apartment upset, reeling from this "new" information. He had believed they were exclusively dating and had been very explicit as to what he was about from the start.

Strangely enough, the last few women he dated had all done the same thing. They all told him they wanted exclusivity, but Brian would later discover that they were dating other men and eventually broke up with him over it. This led him to believe the strength of the story he created about exclusivity, which led him to the conclusion that the relationship with Sara was over. This thrusted Brian into an emotional tailspin that left him battling significant depression. He did not want to get out of bed for days.

A week after their conversation, they finally met and talked about what had happened. Sara confessed that she had spoken poorly and that she was trying to say that she was not ready for the label of "boyfriend and girlfriend." She also clarified that she had only gone on a couple other dates between their first and second date six months ago and nothing since then. Once Brian had his story checked by their discussion, he was excited and grateful about the future possibilities of their relationship. Brian's emotional turmoil could have been avoided if only he had held the position of "I don't know" and been more curious about what she had meant. Instead, it cost him days of not being able to get out of bed—and almost cost him the whole relationship.

The process of accepting and embracing that we *do not know* what people mean, think, or feel is something that will take work before it becomes a natural part of how we experience our world. Taking on the position of

"I don't know" is a conscious effort to release our desire for control in this area of our lives. Holding a position of not knowing might make us anxious at first. But it is much more anxiety-provoking if we choose to continue to hold the position that our meaning-making and stories are actually providing facts. Our stories just offer more anxiety for our emotions to feed on.

Couples can be the worst culprits when it comes to believing they know what their partner is thinking or feeling. A common occurrence with couples is they expect that, after being together for a length of time, they know, or should know, what each other is thinking and feeling. We make statements like, "Wow, you're crabby today," as if we can generalize why they had an edge to how they said something.

We like the idea that another person would know us better than anyone else and have such a deep connection that they understand the *why* behind certain things, but this is just not realistic. The reality is that no matter how long we have been together, people do not fully "know" each other—and this is not a bad thing! People are changing every day, and to say we know what anyone is thinking or feeling today because we knew it yesterday is short-sighted. Sure, we know facts about them, but we cannot tell what that person thinks or feels at any given moment. If our partner tells us something, we need to stay curious about what they mean. We need to recognize just how much our story about others gets in the way of truly knowing them.

Our experience of choosing a stance that embraces "I don't know" is one of willful ignorance. By doing this, we are willfully choosing to ignore the feelings being fed by the story created by our meaning-making. We recognize that getting to the truth will require greater curiosity and exploration than just our own internal interpretations.

LOOKING AHEAD

We have been looking closely at what it can mean to live an empowered life and the impact it can have on our quality of life. In exploring empowerment, we have seen how we have a choice over our attitude, outlook, and our own story and how we choose to understand our experiences. We have discovered what it can mean to be a lifetime learner and how it can help us become the person we want to be instead of a person that lives on autopilot. Lastly, we have learned how empowering and freeing it can be to take an approach to life that embraces the phrase "I don't know" and the vital part it plays in helping us to easily address conflict.

We will now be stepping into a deeper form of empowerment as we explore emotional intelligence and its importance in our experience of addressing conflict in our lives.

Chapter 8

EMOTIONAL INTELLIGENCE

BRIAN AND SARA had their two children immediately after getting married, and they had been through a lot in their seven years together. They loved each other deeply but had never taken the time to focus on their own relationship because of all the other demands on their time. As the years passed and they fell into a routine, Sara struggled with feeling more and more disconnected from Brian. Nothing notable had happened, but she began to feel a distance between them as if they were just roommates, and she did not know why. During this time, Sara found out that her grandmother had passed away, and she was distraught. When she turned to Brian for comfort, he sympathized by expressing how sorry he was that she was going through this. However, Sara did not feel comforted by his words. Coupled with her feelings about their relationship and disconnection, she felt alone—even with his efforts to be there for her.

Brian and Sara's experience is like many of ours—we do not recognize the importance of focusing on the work of developing ourselves or growing our relationships. When we neglect relationships and fall into a routine, we experience disconnection that we struggle to understand, which can lead to feelings of loneliness and isolation, even when we are not alone. One of the keys to developing ourselves and our relationships is our emotional intelligence.

Emotional intelligence is our ability to connect, be in tune with, and regulate our own emotions. It also gives us the insight and ability to understand and respond to other's emotions and feel empathy toward them. We can communicate in a way that builds healthy attached relationships, and we can develop our ability to differentiate our reactive emotional experience from our primary emotions. When we feel the intensity of our reactive emotions, such as frustration and anger, it is difficult for us to slow down and discover what is underneath them that is leading us to these feelings. Emotional intelligence gives us the resources to recognize that we are having an emotional experience, and we can challenge our automatic process of meaning-making and the story that comes out of it.

Through our emotional intelligence, we connect with ourselves and others. Emotional intelligence gives us the ability to hold the space for another's experience instead of just reacting to our own feelings. It allows us to see how much we are influenced by fear, helps us learn to manage our instinctual reactions, and, instead, make meaningful choices about how we want to react to our fear.

Emotional intelligence is one of the keys to our emotional freedom, as it provides us with the ability to perceive, control, and evaluate emotions which, in turn, gives us power over our negative stories and the emotional impacts they have on our lives.

In this chapter, we will discuss emotional intelligence and its various components, as well as its role in addressing conflict both within ourselves and with others. Through a relational framework, we will understand how we see relationships, which in turn, will inform us and help us grow our self-awareness, self-regulation, and empathy.

A RELATIONAL FRAMEWORK

Learning to be aware of our thoughts and feelings is essential in our process of developing emotional intelligence. If we are not aware of why we think or feel the way we do, we will never live an empowered life that encompasses true self-determination. Instead, we will be stuck in a way of being that simply reacts to others without insight or control over why. Self-awareness includes working to recognize the ways in which we *lack* self-awareness, developing an understanding of our inner world and how we view it, embracing the truth of our emotional experience, and allowing ourselves to listen to what our emotions are telling us about what our experiences really mean to us.

When we have self-awareness and start to evaluate our own experiences, we can begin to make choices to self-regulate not only our reactions to others but also our own emotional experiences, including the negative stories that make us feel stuck. By way of reminder, self-regulation is the process of being able to regulate our own thoughts, emotions, and reactions. If we are not aware of why we think or feel what we do, how could we ever choose to regulate how we respond to it? Our work of self-regulation is informed by our ability to understand our own emotions, evaluate the meaning-making we do and the stories that get created by it, and the mindful practices we develop to gain greater insight into ourselves.

Mindfulness works well when we establish relational frameworks about the changes that we are working toward in our lives. For example, if we develop our understanding of anger in a way that defines it as "a reactive emotion that is in defense of a primary emotion," this sets the framework for practicing mindfulness when we are angry or experiencing others' anger. We can then tune into the importance of issues that we are actively working to be mindful of. Choosing to have a perspective that "assumes the best of others" is a frame of mindfulness that can drive us to question the meaning-making that we do, which allows us to choose the positive story we want over our default negative version.

The mindfulness we exercise by taking these concepts and creating the framework that we use in understanding what is happening in relationships will be something that continually grows our emotional intelligence.

A WHOLE NEW WORLD

Emotional intelligence has a direct correlation to the conflicts we experience with ourselves and others, as well as the intensity and impact of these conflicts on us. Unfortunately, lacking connection to what we feel is easily accepted as our normal state of being. This may be due to how little our culture values emotions and continues to provide messages that either "our emotions are not okay" or "we are too emotional." When we hear these messages often, we learn to reject our own emotional experiences, which keeps us from developing our emotional intelligence. The good news is that we can still learn to develop it. This is essential for our work of learning to successfully address conflict.

We need to embrace emotions as a gift that informs us about our actual experiences instead of rejecting them. Emotional intelligence provides meaningful insight about us that, if harnessed, can help us learn to see the true nature of things. If our lens does not include emotional awareness, our default reactive emotions will twist how we see and understand everything. Through emotional intelligence, we can learn to manage our emotional experiences and our reaction to them, which can have a significant impact on the depression and anxiety that happen in response to our stories. And, with emotional intelligence, we gain the ability to address conflict with ease versus escalating it.

Often when we feel like we are being judged or criticized in relationships, we respond by taking a defensive position. For example, if we feel like someone is asserting that we meant something that we did not, we take a defensive position. Similarly, if someone is adamant that we feel a certain way and we do not, we take a defensive position. When we take a defensive position, we usually do two things. First, we put up a protective wall that will not let anything through. Once this wall is in place, we will not hear their logic or be able to understand where they are coming from because we are too busy insisting that they hear *our* truth. We work to explain what we really mean and how what they are saying is wrong.

The minute they feel our defenses go up, others react by erecting their own defensive barrier that will not allow our truths through. They, too, begin their own verbal defense of their position, and we arrive at a stalemate. The negative cycle escalates from there, with both parties erecting protective barriers. We cannot hear each other, and, at the same time, we escalate our verbal approach in our effort to get the other to hear us.

Emotional intelligence opens a new world to us—the inner world, which allows us to shift the paradigm by which we see everything and everyone around us. Instead of interpreting everything based on our meaning-making and the stories we develop, we become self-aware. We can see beyond both what we feel and how we experience others. It empowers us to see people differently and engage their stories as a representation of something deeper that they are trying to express. We can then change our reactions to others from anger to empathy. This new paradigm opens the door to curiosity, knowing that the only way we get to the truth is through the process of discovery.

Instead of seeing someone as angry or frustrated, we begin to see someone who is struggling with emotions that are leading them to reactive behaviors of anger and frustration. When we see this, we can enter the realm of curiosity instead of our natural response of being defensive. We discover emotional freedom when we no longer believe that others' anger or frustration is about us; instead, we recognize that their anger is about something deeper within themselves that they are not in touch with.

The new paradigm of viewing our world through emotional intelligence can be seen in Scott's healthier response to Julie. Historically, Scott has been very quick to hear everything Julie says as a criticism. Earlier, we explored how he negatively interpreted her question, "Did you take the garbage out?" as a criticism. Historically, when she asked him simple questions, his response would be to ascribe negative meaning to what she was asking, which included criticism of himself. The stories Scott told led him to believe that Julie felt a lot of negative things about him. In return, Scott felt miserable and owned a story that he was not enough for Julie; he believed she really did not want to be with him. At the same time, Julie felt like nothing she did or said was right and that she always had to walk on eggshells because she was doing something wrong.

As Julie and Scott continued to work on their relationship, they developed their emotional intelligence. Scott was able to realize that he had a default lens of criticism that shaped his interpretation of his wife. This lens had led him to interpret the most mundane things as if she was criticizing him. He came to understand how he had developed this critical lens in response to his upbringing as the youngest of three who felt disregarded.

Scott still quickly interprets comments or questions as criticism, but now he is armed with this new framework of understanding. When he feels his critical story come alive in response to his wife, he can mindfully recognize the interpretation and hold it as a story instead of his truth. This has given him the space to check his critical story with his wife instead of owning it. By doing this, Scott has been able to take the conflict he experiences and use mindfulness and emotional intelligence to help him control his interpretations and response to it. He now uses conflict as a place to reach for connection with Julie and for the two of them to grow their attachment to one another. As we see from Scott's experience, there is a relationship between mindfulness and emotional intelligence.

MINDFULNESS AS A LIFESTYLE

Mindfulness is a key factor in emotional intelligence. It is the active practice of having a nonjudgmental awareness of our thoughts, emotions, and experiences on a moment-by-moment basis. The practice of active awareness helps us determine why we think, feel, and interpret things the way we do. Mindfulness is a process of slowing down and exploring the meaning we are making of a situation. Slowing down helps us gain awareness of our motivations and leads us to empowerment in our choices.

Let's think of a couple of concrete examples of practicing mindfulness. Imagine approaching a five-way-stop intersection while driving in a busy city and getting anxious. By taking the time to slow down and work to understand what we are experiencing, we discover that we are feeling anxious because of the fear of the chaos and unpredictability of what everyone else will do at the intersection. We feel powerless and out of control in that moment. Another example is when we are having a discussion with a friend and immediately have a strong emotional reaction to what they are saying. We have an autopilot response, not even thinking about why we feel this way. If we are mindful, we recognize the intensity of our defensiveness and slow down to ask ourselves why we are feeling so defensive. We discover we have interpreted what they were saying as if they were criticizing us, and then we realize that we do not know what they meant by what they were saying. We can choose to adopt a position of curiosity and recognize that we need more information from them to understand what they are trying to communicate.

Mindfulness is vital to recognizing the truth of our experiences. As we learn to accept our emotions as vital information and develop our mindfulness about them, it can provide insight into what our emotions are truly trying to reveal about our inner world. In fact, it is crucial for us to even recognize the most basic aspect of our emotions—that we are experiencing them! From there, we can learn to tune into the interplay between reactive and primary emotions. When we are angry or frustrated about something, mindfulness helps us slow down and discover the primary emotion behind these reactive ones. Then it allows us to discover what it is that is driving these defensive positions in the first place.

Mindfulness grows our emotional intelligence, as it allows us to tune into how and why we interpret our experiences the way that we do. We tend to feel emotions and respond to them without first asking why we are feeling what we do. As we accept, appreciate, and understand the difference between reactive and primary emotions, we come to see that our way out of stuck reactive emotional experiences is through emotional mindfulness. We can then tune into the primary emotions behind them. This also includes slowing down. In the process of mindfulness, we need to ask important questions of ourselves. These questions allow us to understand our ideologies and why we think and feel the way we do about things, which can allow us to realign our perspectives.

When we lack self-awareness, we might fight to control things in our lives without taking the time to evaluate why we want to control them or whether we can or should have control over them. The ways we attempt control often cause us more harm than if we had just accepted the situation at hand. We should be engaging our mindfulness and asking the questions necessary to understand our situation, such as:

- What is motivating me to want control?
- Is this really something I/we can control?
- Is how we are trying to control the situation good for us or making things worse in other ways?

Without practicing mindfulness, our attempts to control things can lead to greater harm and suffering for ourselves and our relationships. *With* mindfulness, we can evaluate and develop healthy and meaningful control over the factors in life that we *do* have influence over. Doing so can improve how we think and feel about ourselves and our relationships.

FROM CONFLICT TO DISCOVERY

Mindfulness is also central to our process of addressing conflict. As we learn to understand why we think and feel the way we do, we glean the insight and empowerment to own our thoughts and actions. This leads us to a place of being able to address conflict in a positive way that creates connection with others. It gives us the space to see emotions as information about ourselves and others, which can allow us to move past our world of reactions and engage with curiosity.

When we experience conflict with another person, it is easy to react to their words or behaviors and feel attacked, criticized, or judged. Slowing down and being mindful gives us the power to set aside these feelings and our need to react to them. Through mindfulness, we can go to questions of curiosity such as:

- Why are they saying what they are?
- What meaning-making and story do they have right now?
- What might they be afraid of that is leading them to have such a strong reaction?

We are usually quick to define what is happening with someone based on how *we feel* about the interaction. When we mindfully engage curiosity, it turns this process on its head. We can focus on understanding the real experience instead of our story about what others are thinking and feeling.

When we slow down and take time to be mindful, conflict becomes a place of discovery. We learn about ourselves and what matters to us as we grow in our understanding of our feelings and the thoughts that are impacting them. In relationships, mindfulness can allow us to see and accept different perspectives without being stuck in our singular self-focused lens. We become aware of and work to understand how others experience the world and even how they experience us. This gives us the focus and ability to see beyond our own perspective.

The process of developing mindfulness starts from a belief that our natural interpretation of things is often inaccurate. It is the process of slowing down and taking time to ask ourselves questions such as:

- Why do I think this?
- What am I feeling?
- How does this thought make me feel?
- Why am I choosing to do what I am?

At the core, mindfulness means developing a deep sense of curiosity about ourselves. We can enhance our mindfulness through slowing down, self-affirmations, grounding practices, meditation, creating frameworks of understanding, paying attention to emotions coming alive, and taking time to ask curious questions before reacting.

EMPATHY:
THE RELATIONAL SUPERPOWER

An essential component of developing emotional intelligence is empathy. Developing empathy directly correlates to our level of emotional intelligence; we cannot have one without the other, as they are two sides of the same coin. We should see empathy as emotional intelligence in action. Our emotional intelligence gives us the ability to recognize others' emotions, and our engagement of empathy takes this recognition and applies it to deep understanding and connection with their emotional experience.

Empathy is the process of allowing ourselves to feel, experience, and understand the thoughts and feelings of another person. It is a positive assumption that works to place us in someone else's emotional experience and connect with them. Empathy is not about developing an ability to assume we know what they feel; it is about trying to see if our interpretation of their emotional experience is in tune with them. Empathy is about connecting with someone on an emotional level, not just an intellectual or logical one.

Empathy and emotions are closely linked, and both can often be devalued in different ways. When our culture devalues emotions by saying they are "not okay to have" or calling us "too emotional," the value of empathy also gets distorted. We all want others to be empathetic toward us, but often we think it is unnecessary to be empathetic to others—or we just do not know how to provide empathy to them, and we get upset when they want it from us.

Often in life, we engage others from the position of sympathy instead of empathy, likely because we really do not want to know or already think we do know what others are feeling. The problem with sympathy is how disconnected it is from the other person and what they are going through.

As we look back at Brian and Sara's experience of Sara's grandmother's passing, we see how Brian tried to comfort his wife by sympathizing with her experience. He expressed how bad he felt for her loss, and she appreciated this, but she did not feel comforted in the way she had hoped.

When Sara shared her loss with her best friend Cindy, Cindy connected with her emotions, imagining what it would be like to lose her own grandmother. She was curious about Sara's relationship with her grandmother and was able to connect with what it must be like for Sara to go through the loss. With this insight and understanding of her own emotions, Cindy was able to share her sadness at the deep pain Sara must have been feeling and sat in these emotions with her. Sara's spirits were lifted by someone seeing her and her suffering, which provided a deep connection that made her feel less alone. Cindy's response was in contrast to what she experienced from Brian. Brian expressed sympathy but did not have the empathy that Sara desired to have her emotional experience feel seen and understood. The result of his lack of empathy was Sara feeling a significant disconnection from Brian.

When we lack empathy, the people around us feel unseen and experience us as if we do not care about them in a meaningful way. Even when we express how bad we feel for others, our words fall flat. Our words of support do not express our care when we are disconnected from their emotional experience. We are not connecting with them on an emotional level within ourselves. We struggle to build trust and support with others, and it leaves us feeling just as disconnected as if we had been in a negative relational cycle with them.

HOW TO DEVELOP EMPATHY

Empathy is both a key component of emotional intelligence and created by it. Empathy requires being mindful of our emotions *and* the emotions of others. It requires developing our emotional intelligence to be able to tune into what we feel and what another's emotional experience might feel like.

It's easy to dismiss empathy and fail to recognize how important it really is to our ability to feel valued by others. If we go through life having our emotional experience dismissed—either directly by people's messages or indirectly by their inability to engage our emotional experience—we can feel incredibly isolated and alone, even if we are surrounded by a massive family and community.

The challenge in developing empathy is learning to ask questions about ourselves and others, such as:

- What would it be like to have what happened to another person happen to me?
- How would it impact me?
- How would I feel in response to it?
- What would it feel like for me to be in their position?

We all have the ability to develop empathy since it already exists to some degree within each of us. We experience empathy every time we watch a movie or television show and feel the emotions of the characters. We fear the impending doom of the storyline or the excitement of someone finding true love. Believing we do not have empathy becomes a good excuse for not wanting to put in the effort needed to develop it.

As we work to develop our empathy, we need to first learn to embrace emotions and work to tune into our own emotional experiences. We must learn to allow ourselves to imagine what it would be like for us to go through what another person has and allow ourselves to feel the emotions that would come alive in response to it. The effort that we put into developing our empathy will pay us back with deeper connections to others and an enhanced ability to develop meaningful, lasting relationships.

If we are unwilling to embrace emotions and allow ourselves to truly feel them in our own lives, we will never be able to have true empathy for another. The depth of our empathy is directly dependent on how deep we are willing to go into our own emotions and fears. We may have no problem connecting with the *positive* emotions of others, but we will never understand someone's pain and suffering if we continually refuse to feel it in ourselves—or even acknowledge its existence.

Our fear of facing certain emotions keeps us from living a full life. Since our first step in changing is acceptance of our own emotions, it is important for us to recognize we can handle it. These emotions will not kill us. As a matter of fact, they already exist within us. We might as well make ourselves whole by accepting them. As we learn to accept and integrate our own emotional experiences, it can lead us to a deeper understanding of ourselves and deeper connections with others through empathy.

MOVING FORWARD

Emotional intelligence is important because it gives us the resources and understanding we need to know and manage our own emotions. It provides us with the ability to manage ourselves in response to how we experience the emotions of others, and it informs us in a way that allows us to hear what others are saying, even when they are communicating critically. It is one of the main tools that enables us to recognize the dynamics at play in our relationships and respond to them in a constructive way. Emotional intelligence leads us to greater connection with others instead of more conflict. However, more important than emotional intelligence itself is the effort we take to develop it in our lives.

We are all unique and must decide for ourselves what the journey to develop our emotional intelligence looks like. But this journey will require consistency, determination, and a vision that acknowledges how emotional intelligence helps us become better at being in relationships. This emotional intelligence will lead us to empathy and will develop our ability to connect with others on a deeper emotional level. It will also assist us in our awareness of our own emotions, interpretations, and the management of our stories. As we learn to engage our inner world, we can take ownership of our thought processes and the emotional impacts they have on us. We will also be better prepared to see others with insight and empathy instead of judgment and criticism.

This journey requires our determination to change and become more than we are today. We must accept our emotions and develop our ability to tune into them. We must aspire to be better at relationships and grow them to their fullest potential through our understanding of relational dynamics and a vision for developing secure attachment within them. Ultimately, the journey requires our determination to grow and change in a way that helps us to be the person we desire to be in relationships: a person who can easily address conflict and find connection out of our differences.

So far, in this journey of learning how to address conflict, we have seen how we are intrinsically different from others and view our experiences as such, how we fill in the gaps of our understanding with our meaning-making and false stories, and how our reactive emotions quickly drive our reactive behaviors. The factors we have covered highlight the importance of being more explicit in our communication. In the next chapter, we will see how being explicit is essential for improving our communication, reducing misunderstandings, and addressing conflict.

Chapter 9

THE VALUE OF BEING EXPLICIT

BRIAN HAS BEEN working a high-pressure job as a manager for a tech company. The pace is fast, and he spends so much time in meetings that it leaves very little time to get his daily work done. Brian prides himself on being a good leader and always trying to encourage his team—he values them as individuals, understands how challenging their work environment is, and tries to show support as much as possible.

Against a big deadline for a new product launch, Brian's manager calls him into his office. He berates Brian because his team is not making enough progress, and he makes it crystal clear that Brian's team could *not* miss the deadline.

After the conversation finished, with tensions high, Brian walked directly into his own team meeting. As he entered the conference room, still reeling from being chewed out by his manager, he immediately jumped in. "You guys are nowhere near finishing this on time, and I've had it!" He fumed. "We're all going to put in extra hours to meet this deadline, you hear me?"

Once the meeting was over, Brian's team commiserated about what a jerk Brian was being. "He must think we're incompetent, right? I mean, he hasn't even recognized any of the hard work we've put toward this. He's just focusing on the shortcomings and not seeing how hard we've been pushing for the deadline." They were frustrated because there were factors outside of their control that contributed to the tight timeline, but they were being criticized as if it was *their* fault they were behind. As a result, morale was low, and the team members spent a good deal of time discussing their dissatisfaction with their company and the leadership rather than being motivated to get the work done.

If we pay attention to how we speak with one another, we will quickly discover that we bring up many things in conversation that we leave others to interpret. And even though we often communicate in a vague way, others seldom ask clarifying questions. Thus, we assume that other people understand the meaning we intended, and they assume they know what we mean. But this might not be the case! We automatically define our understanding of what other people are saying by the meaning-making we do in response to what we hear. We make assumptions that can lead to misunderstandings.

In the situation above, Brian did not explicitly share with the team his thoughts about all the good work they had done up until that point. The truth was, he was proud of their work, and he knew they were coming against factors outside of their control. But he had come into the conference room projecting his frustrated energy from the meeting with his manager. Though he valued his team's hard work to meet the deadline, he didn't share that with them. Instead, he gave them the impression he was upset and needed even more out of them—which, in turn, left them making meaning about what he thought of them. In the same way that he never expressed his thoughts and feelings directly to them, they also never asked him how he felt about their performance so far. Instead, they just took their interpretation of his energy, the pressure he was putting on them to meet the deadline, and what was not said as the basis of their understanding of how he viewed them.

This leads me to the main point of this chapter: the value of being explicit. Being explicit is our opportunity to clearly communicate what we mean or how we feel without relying on doubt or assumptions. Being explicit is crucial to growing connections and nurturing attachment with others. It is essential in our efforts to address conflicts when they arise, and being explicit is one of the greatest forces in preventing conflict altogether. My goal is to help all of us become open and clear communicators with others who let them know *specifically* what we think and feel. This requires us to assume that others do not know what we are thinking or feeling unless we tell them. Explicitness allows us to be seen and understood, and it helps us avoid the stories people create about us when they do not know what to think. In that way, it also works to avoid conflict. In the following sections, we will look at the power of assumptions and what being explicit looks like in different relationships in our lives.

ASSUMPTIONS: USE THEM FOR GOOD

A common experience we all likely relate to is when someone responds to the question "How are you doing?" with a simple, automatic answer, "Good." This response tells us almost nothing, yet we immediately assume how they are doing based on our interpretation of what "good" means to us. Often, we do not even think of asking, "Why are you good?" or "What do you mean by good?"

When we settle for "good" as an explanation for how someone is doing, we lose the chance to more deeply understand who they are. More than this, we lose the opportunity for a greater connection and a more secure attachment in our relationship with them. This daily experience is a perfect example of mutual assumptions.

Taking things one step further, negative assumptions often lead us into conflict and cause damage to relationships. We assume we know what others think, feel, or mean by what they say, and then we own it as truth. Subsequently, we are left dealing with the emotional impact of this "truth" in our lives. Our assumptions limit our curiosity and make us feel comfortable shutting off, believing we already know things that we do not.

Luckily, we do not need to be bound by the emotions that our negative assumptions create in us. Some assumptions can allow us to connect with others and grow our attachment. For example, intentional *positive* assumptions can permit us to frame our understanding in a way that gives us control over our reactions and emotional experiences. This type of positive assumption can be as simple as "assuming the best of others." If we assume the best of others, these assumptions create positive words and behaviors in response. Instead of assuming the worst, we approach our relationships from a position of hope, which has a positive impact on how others experience us and how we feel about them.

Another approach to positive assumptions in relational dynamics is assuming "I do not know what you mean" or that the anger or frustration someone exhibits "is about something else." When we can hold these relational assumptions open, it can drive us to a greater understanding of others. If we recognize that we do not know what others mean by their words, it allows us the space to enter with curiosity and work toward a deeper understanding. In this same way, positively assuming that others' expressions of anger and frustration are about something else, such as their primary emotion, rather than being about us, allows us to regulate our own emotional responses. Taking this approach allows us to move from an emotional position of reacting to their possible anger or frustration to a position of empathy for the things, like fear, that might be leading them to their reactive feelings.

We have started our exploration of explicitness by first looking at assumptions for a simple reason. By understanding the power of our assumptions and how easily we create them, we can see more clearly the importance and value of being explicit. Being explicit leads us to greater connection with others and often stops conflict before it starts.

FAMILY MATTERS

Family is one of the most challenging places for us to be explicit due to the way we accept family dynamics as a normal way of interacting. We often do not even think of questioning our family dynamics until we are far enough away from them to recognize what they really are. This way of seeing the world limits our understanding that we need to be straightforward with others, especially with our own family.

Many of us believe that being explicit is bad or wrong—that if we express our feelings, thoughts, or love for one another too often, it will lose its meaning. Often this belief comes from our upbringing and what was modeled by caregivers. If we grew up in a home where our primary caregivers did not explicitly tell us how they felt, we may have adopted this approach as normal. Our tendency to avoid being direct can also be a result of wanting to be loved and never getting a clear message about our value from the people who mattered most. When this happens, we can end up believing that it is unnecessary or even wrong to share feelings explicitly and too often.

The importance of explicitness between parents and children about their thoughts and feelings is essential in developing emotional intelligence. Parents can have an amazing impact on their children by simply explicitly sharing their thoughts and feelings and being curious about their children. An example of this is when parents are vulnerable and share emotions of sadness or fear with their children and model a healthy way to integrate and regulate their emotions. Another example is a parent's efforts to set aside their own interpretation of their child's extreme emotions and instead be curious and explore their child's emotional experience. By working to gain an understanding of their child's inner world, they will validate his or her emotions and help develop their emotional intelligence. They will also cultivate a secure attachment between them and their child that produces safety, security, and the freedom to take risks in life.

We often take relationships with siblings, like family in general, for granted. We look at siblings as being in our life based solely on the fact that we are related. However, our childhood relationships leave a lasting impact on how we view each other and our strongly ingrained stories about who we believe each other to be. We assume that we know who our siblings are, and we believe they know us. Because of this, we often do not feel it necessary to explicitly express our thoughts and feelings or be curious about theirs. This leaves us only knowing a caricature of our siblings. We often never really get to know who they are today or have a meaningful relationship based on curiosity about what they think and feel.

NOW, ASK YOURSELF:

- What leads you to be curious (or not) about your family?
- How concrete is your understanding of who your family members are?
- What kind of assumptions are you making about your family?
- In what ways do your assumptions about your family keep you from being curious?
- Do you ever show curiosity about your family members' thoughts or feelings to them directly?

Challenges with direct communication can also be seen with our extended family, as these dynamics can be loaded with a great deal of judgment and criticism, combined with a lack of regular contact. This combination can leave a relational distance and offer us limited knowledge and understanding of one another. At the same time, we take great leaps in our assumptions due to our place in our family. Extended family members can often feel entitled to speak into our lives and choices without ever developing a relationship where they really know us. We can end up hiding our true selves from our family, not knowing how to be explicit with them due to the unsafe emotional nature of these relationships. We may not feel that we can live an authentic life with extended family.

Difficulties can also occur for the opposite reason. When we assume that just because people are family, we should be vulnerable and share our thoughts and feelings, this can prevent us from guarding ourselves from relationships that might be unsafe. We give them the privilege of our thoughts and feelings strictly because of their positioning as family, not because they have proven to be deserving of these parts of us. Tim's experience helps to illustrate these points.

Tim grew up in a large core and extended family with a culture that valued being in the military above everything. Tim wanted nothing more than for his family to be proud of him, so in the third grade, he told his family that he wanted to be a Navy Seal. The entire family's response was excitement for his interest, and he quickly became the favorite among the children because of it. As time went on and he entered high school, he came to realize he had no interest in being in the military. This led Tim into an intense emotional tailspin. He felt that if he told his family he did not want to be in the military, they would no longer be proud of him. He feared that they would be disappointed in him, and he did not believe he could handle the rejection.

Tim's inability to explicitly share his thoughts and feelings about his life goals caused him to feel emotionally distraught. In fact, the idea of letting his family down and not having them be proud of him led to thoughts of suicide. He finally opened up to a friend who encouraged him to share with his family what he was going through. Though his family expressed feelings of disappointment, Tim was able to begin a journey of discovering his passions instead of just doing what would make him feel accepted by his family. Over time, Tim learned how to explicitly share his own thoughts and feelings and differentiate his desires from his family's in a way that made him more confident in himself.

Explicitly sharing thoughts and feelings can ultimately become a place of empowerment, as we can see in Tim's experience. Empowerment led him to deeper relationships with those in his family who could see and value him for who he was. It also alienated him from people who wanted him to live out their expectations. In the end, it left him with a greater sense of who he was, and he took ownership of his own journey in life.

Too often, we feel like Tim—stuck being defined by the assumptions of our family, which causes us to feel unseen for who we really are. In turn, we can easily do the same and think we know who our family members are, which keeps us from ever being curious about their thoughts or feelings. This just highlights the importance of learning to communicate in a straightforward way. Additionally, due to our tendency to assume, we must remember how much more important it is to be explicit the closer and more central the relationships are.

LOVE THE ONES YOU'RE WITH

Once we leave our family of origin, partners are often our primary relationships. In these relationships, it is important that we work to create secure attachment by developing healthy ways of addressing conflict. A key to addressing, and even avoiding, conflict is to develop our ability to be explicit about our thoughts and feelings and work with our partners to do the same.

In these relationships, we can also get stuck believing that our partner should know how we feel because we have previously informed them of our feelings. We think that because we shared the depth of how much we care for them—at *some* point in history—that they know it is an unchanging reality. The minute we think we know what our partner thinks or feels, we are in for a rough ride. These assumptions are catastrophic because we are all constantly changing. Just because we knew what our partner thought or felt about something yesterday, last week, or last year does not make it true at this moment. In this same way, our partners do not know how we think or feel unless we explicitly share it with them.

In fact, as time moves forward, many of our words and actions send messages that can be perceived as contrary to what we once made clear. When our partners continually perceive negative messages from our body language and behaviors, our previous communication of love cannot compete with the mountain of contrary experiences tipping our partner's emotional scales toward not feeling loved. We may dearly love our partner; we have just stopped doing the work necessary to make our love crystal clear in consistent ways. The reason to be explicit with our partners is to grow our attachment to one another as a place of safety, security, and vulnerability. This is done through all forms of clarity in sharing our thoughts and feelings.

Brian's experience of explicitly sharing his feelings is a simple example. Brian had just arrived home from work one day, and he wanted to sit down and relax, but he knew he needed to clean up the kitchen first. As he took the garbage outside, he was thinking about how frustrated he was with having to do these tedious tasks. When he came back into the house, he was surprised to find that his wife Sara had replaced the garbage bag in the house can. Sara is a very kind and thoughtful person who is always doing things for Brian. He shows his appreciation, but it almost always ends with just a "thank you."

At this moment, when Sara replaced the garbage bag so that he did not have to, Brian felt an overwhelming appreciation for her, and his love overflowed. Instead of just saying "thank you" like normal, Brian recognized this was an opportunity for him to grow attachment with Sara. "When I came back in from taking out the trash and noticed that you replaced the bag, it made me feel deeply loved. I want you to know how much it means to me, honey. Thank you," he said, looking into her eyes.

Sara had always felt like he appreciated what she did for him, but the overflow of love and direct communication was not how she normally experienced him. To know that her actions made him feel loved in this way was a whole new level of being able to understand his thoughts and feelings and the impact of her actions. This made her happy and feel seen in a deeper way than a simple "thank you" would have ever done.

NOW, ASK YOURSELF:

- How often do you think something meaningful about another person but do not share it?
- What opportunities have you missed to be explicit with someone?
- How can you start to be more explicit with people that matter to you?
- How might you grow your attachment with someone by being more explicit?

Another area where explicitness is often overlooked is dating. Clear communication is our greatest asset if we desire to protect our heart and the other person from the harm that can come out of our assumptions. However, dating is often the area where we are the most afraid to be explicit. We want our partner to like us, and too often, our fear of rejection leads us to act in a way that we think the other person will like. In our effort to be accepted, instead of being ourselves, we try to be something and someone we are not. This fear keeps us from being explicit and sharing what we are thinking and feeling, and we miss the opportunity to build a safe connection with the other person from the start.

One of the results of not being clear is that we rely on perception and assumptions to inform us of how the relationship is going. Amy's experience offers one example. Amy had been dating Jake for a short time, and they had gone from being casual friends to being intimate over the past month. Amy was evaluating the possibilities of the relationship and still viewed it as casual, even though they had become physical. She had not shared much about her thoughts and feelings, especially about the relationship itself, for fear of how she might possibly be rejected. She just wanted to hold onto the excitement of the new relationship and how good it was feeling as she worked to discover if she saw a future for them. Her only tool for evaluating her experience was how it felt, and she still did not know.

After a month of dating, they had a conversation about the relationship, and Amy discovered that Jake had high hopes and expectations for the relationship. Unfortunately, he was in a much different place than she was. Once she learned where he thought the relationship was going, it triggered her fears of causing him deeper pain in the future if she was unable to get to where he already was.

Amy and Jake's lack of explicitness about their thoughts and feelings in the first month led each of them to different assumptions about the relationship. Once Amy recognized that they were not at the same level, she felt stuck, like something was wrong with her. She feared she was causing him greater harm each day she let the relationships continue. She felt like her only solution to minimize the pain at this point was to end the relationship, which she quickly did. This hurt him deeply and left her feeling like an awful person, and she questioned herself and her ability to be a good partner for someone.

All of this might have been avoided if they had been explicit from the beginning. If they had shared their thoughts and feelings about the relationship on an ongoing basis, they could have kept it in check. Neither of them would have had a chance to run too far ahead of the other. The outcome might have been different.

NOW, ASK YOURSELF:

- How has your lack of explicitness led to assumptions like Amy experienced?
- When and how have you experienced conflict in relationships because of a lack of explicitness?
- What are a few ways you can be more explicit in your relationship(s)?

Explicitness may not be our default way to relate to our partners, but it is a gift that allows us to change our interactions and leads to greater connection at every stage. The more we learn to explicitly share our thoughts and feelings, the less conflict we will experience due to the vagueness that keeps us trapped in ignorance.

FRIENDSHIPS NEED WORK, TOO

Aside from our primary relationships with our family or a partner, friends are extremely important. For those of us who do not have a partner or who have a challenging family life, friends can be our primary relationships. In effect, they become the family of our choosing. No matter what our other relationships are, being in a community and having friends play an important role in our quality of life and sense of belonging. Because having healthy friendships is important, it is essential we learn how to be explicit with our friends if we want to preserve and deepen our relationships.

It is easy for us to assume the meaning of our friends' words or actions and then create a negative story about what they were thinking or feeling. When we do not have enough self-awareness to be explicit, we can act out and cause serious harm to our relationships, maybe even alienating our friends and losing them altogether. An example of this can be seen in an interaction Brian had.

Brian, Chris, and two other men had been friends ever since college. They decided to take a three-day hiking trip deep into the mountains. Brian was an over-planner and packed a lot of supplies, including one of the tents, making his pack very heavy and the fifteen-mile trek challenging. However, after the initial hike, the weekend went smoothly, and they all had a great time.

As they went to pack up the camp, Brian began to put all the supplies he hauled back into his pack. As he did this, he noticed that Chris was just loading his own clothes and sleeping bag into his pack. At this moment, Brian realized that he had carried the weight of supplies for everyone to use, and Chris had only carried his own supplies in a bag that wasn't even full. As Brian continued to pack, critical thoughts about Chris began to fester inside of him, which led Brian to an intense, angry outburst. Brian projected his angry story about Chris's selfishness at him. After some awkward moments of poorly communicating about the issues, Chris took on some of the supplies Brian was carrying, and they made their way off the mountain.

Brian's reactive behaviors in response to his story about Chris's selfishness caused a rift in their relationship, and they spoke very little from that point forward. Brian could have easily been more explicit about his need for Chris to carry more weight as they packed up instead of feeding feelings of judgment in the story he created about Chris's character or intent. Chris felt blindsided by

Brian because he did not even realize that Brian wanted any assistance, or else he would have happily jumped in.

Another way we struggle to be explicit is how we respond to friends asking if we want to do something with them. Many of us often default to saying yes, even if we do not want to do the proposed activity. We say yes out of fear that if we say no, eventually, they will stop asking. It's true: if we do continually say no, it is normal for friends to stop asking. The problem here is that we feel like we need to give a yes or no answer. We never even consider there is another option. In reality, we can offer an explicit answer that shares our thoughts and feelings about the friendship itself. We can even answer the question with a no while also communicating what we want the other person to know about how we think and feel about them and their invitation. For example, we might say, "No, thank you. But I want you to know how much your friendship means to me. I really hope you will continue to ask me to do things." This gives a powerful message of appreciation for our friend's effort and indicates that we would like it to continue in the future.

A lack of explicitness leaves a void of understanding that can negatively impact our friendships. As we look back at the story of Brian and Chris, each filled in the blanks with their own understanding. This left Brian feeling taken advantage of and Chris avoiding Brian because he felt attacked by Brian's judgments. This can also be seen in our example of responding to a friend's invitation.

When we just say no to a friend asking us to do something with them, or even say no with an excuse, they have no understanding about how we feel about them. So, they will fill this void with their own meaning-making and maybe a negative story. We might initially get the benefit of the doubt, but after a couple of "no" responses, their negative story about us not wanting to spend time with them is established and gets affirmed with every new "no."

Living a life that is not explicit or direct leaves space for friends to interpret and create their own negative stories about us. Our meaning-making is often small enough that it never comes to the surface, but it still has an impact on how we perceive our friends and how they perceive us. It ends up tainting and defining the relationship for us instead of us creating greater connections through more explicit communication.

WORKPLACE COMMUNICATION

Explicitly sharing our thoughts is essential in the workplace, but it looks different than it does with partners, family, or friends. Relationships in the workplace are not inherently personal; most of us do not have the luxury of choosing who we want to work with or have as clients. Relationships at work are there to serve the needs of our employer, and we depend on them for our success and our livelihood. These relationships require an explicitness that is clear and concise while avoiding expressing the feelings we would prioritize in our personal relationships. There is a place to express feelings, but in a professional setting, we should not expect the emotional vulnerability we experience in our personal relationships. The impersonal nature of work often leaves so much room for interpretation. The workplace is task-oriented, and the work culture may not leave much time for explicitly communicating with others. In fact, it may take more work to figure out the right way to directly communicate, given that the demands of the work environment may even require us to minimize our interactions.

But, for most of us, our jobs either impact or are impacted by those we work with. This can lead us to criticize and blame quickly, often out of our own fear about how we might be seen by others. As we check our understanding of others, we can avoid getting stuck in our own created beliefs about what others think and feel about us. As we get curious and learn to see from others' perspectives, we develop ways of influencing the stories others have about us. By being explicit, we can remove the power of interpretation and its impact on our communication.

Our ability to explicitly share our thoughts is impacted by the nature of the work environment and the power dynamics that come with it. Since some people have power over others, we must approach each relationship differently. If we are in a position of power over others, this position alone allows the things we say and do, as well as the things we do not clearly communicate, to greatly impact others. The more we can communicate clearly, the more positive the impact we have on people's satisfaction and productivity in the workplace. If we are not careful and explicit, people might make up stories about us and about how we feel or think about the staff. When we are in the position of being subordinate to someone else's authority, it can be easy to get stuck in toxic stories about them that grow until the only escape is to find another job. We can manage our meaning-making by practicing direct communication and working to explicitly share and check our stories and not allow them to have power over our quality of life.

Work relationships can get particularly messy when we end up working with friends or family. In these instances, we are in dual relationships that require different things from us at the same time. This makes the possibility of being explicit both easier and more difficult at times. Because of the nature of the dual relationship, we may feel safe to be vulnerable and share with friends or family that we work with in a way that goes beyond the professional. But it might also be more difficult to differentiate our roles if we are not explicit about the nature of the dual relationship and struggles. We can end up focusing on wanting validation of our emotional experience when the situation might require us to be explicit only about our thoughts and the facts.

Whether with our manager, co-worker, or client, only we can clearly communicate the reality of *our* experience. It is on us to be explicit about what we are thinking and feeling so others can have a clear understanding of our efforts toward our common goals.

MOVING FORWARD

As shown throughout this chapter, how we communicate our thoughts and feelings impacts how we are understood. When there is a lack of explicitness in communication, we can get stuck in our meaning-making and the negative stories created by it. While we cannot completely avoid the meaning-making of others, being straightforward about our thoughts and feelings can strongly reduce misunderstandings. Beyond simply avoiding this negative dynamic of false interpretation, being explicit in our communication is an easy way for us to build secure attachment with others and grow our relationships into safe places of vulnerability. Explicitness is a major tool in our efforts to address conflict, which we will see in the next chapter as we explore the implementation of The Confident Communication Model.

Chapter 10

RESOLVING CONFLICT THROUGH CURIOSITY AND CONNECTION

EVERYTHING WE HAVE covered so far is essential for developing the right mindset to implement The Confident Communication Model. We learned about how we interpret our world and the relational dynamics that occur. These concepts are foundational in shifting our mindset to have more awareness of ourselves and others so we can think and act in more thoughtful and curious ways, particularly in moments that typically lead to conflict.

The Confident Communication Model is a tool to help us understand what we and others are doing as we engage in relationships. It helps us identify the conflict that happens both within ourselves and with others, often due to our own meaning-making or others' meaning-making about us. Most importantly, it shifts our understanding to lead us toward curiosity to discover why we behave the way we do and to reconsider how we affect others.

Once we can understand why we behave the way we do, The Confident Communication Model provides us with a new paradigm that focuses on curiosity about others through building connections. The model helps us develop new ways to see ourselves and the dynamics we face in our relationships with others. The model consists of three components: recognize, evaluate, and address. We start with the most pivotal step, working to simply **recognize** that we are in conflict. We then move on to **evaluate,** which helps us look at our internal experience of the conflict, our reactive and primary emotions related to it, and the meaning-making and story that we create in response to it. We finish with **address,** in which we first decide if the conflict can be addressed within ourselves or if we need to address it with others. Then we do just that: address the conflict. As we learn to implement the model and live it on a daily basis, we will find ourselves experiencing less relational anxieties and see our relationships flourishing in new ways—with greater connectedness and security.

This model lays the groundwork for changing how we see and interpret our relationships, manage our emotional experiences, and empower ourselves to choose what to believe. In fact, this model stresses our ability to "not know" and instead approach situations with curiosity, which provides ways for us to address conflicts easily.

STEP 1: RECOGNIZE

The first step in The Confident Communication Model is to **recognize** conflict. This step is crucial because it allows us to evaluate our response to it and develop meaningful ways to address it. The "recognize" step of The Confident Communication Model is simultaneously the simplest and the hardest step because it requires us to recognize that we are experiencing conflict.

Many of us experience conflict without ever naming it as such, and it takes some work to develop our ability to recognize it. Often, we do not recognize we are in conflict until it rises to a level where we are aggressively attacking one another. The reality is that conflict often happens much more subtly every day. When we go back to our original working definition of conflict as "the presence of difference," we can see that we experience conflict in many interactions with other people because we cannot avoid the intrinsic differences between us.

The easiest way to recognize conflict is by recognizing our own emotional experience. This starts with accepting and embracing our emotions, which becomes essential as we work to allow them to inform us about our meaning-making. We can realize we are in conflict by simply acknowledging our reactive emotions. If we are feeling anxiety, anger, jealousy, resentment, or frustration, we are in conflict. We can also recognize conflict by tuning into the physical sensations our bodies experience, which can become a clear indicator.

However, recognizing we are in conflict is not just about recognizing our own perceptions or reactions to conflict. It is also important to acknowledge when others may have an issue with us, which leads us to be in conflict because of *their* issues. In instances like these, we are in conflict with another person because of how we experience their reactive emotions, meaning-making, or story, or if we experience an energy shift from them. If we do not recognize the conflict others have with us, we will develop conflict anyway as we are triggered to react to their thinking and the behaviors that follow.

Recognizing Conflict Through Our Physical Sensations

Physical sensation is an invaluable way to recognize that we are in conflict. An example of this can be seen in Amy's experience. During her junior year of college, Amy had been going on dates with a man named James for about a month, and things seemed to be going well. It was early in the process of getting to know him, and she was still trying to figure out their potential as a couple. In late September, they went to a bistro where they could sit outside in the warm fall air. The atmosphere was romantic, and Amy was really enjoying herself. She was relaxed and had positive feelings about James and the possibilities of a future with him.

As they discussed their week and the challenges of school, the conversation turned to the next few months and the holidays. During this discussion, James expressed how excited he was for Amy to fly across the country and meet his mom at Thanksgiving. Amy thought it was nice that he would want her to meet his mom. But then she started to feel off: Her stomach started to churn, and she felt tension rise in her shoulders and neck. She did not know what was going on but realized that her body was trying to tell her something. As she slowed her thoughts down and worked to be mindful of why she was feeling the way she was, she began to understand that she was having an internal conflict.

As she pondered the emotional sensations that had come alive, Amy realized she was uncomfortable with the idea of making such meaningful plans when she was still unsure of any future with James. Not only did her physical reaction inform her that she had conflict within herself, but also that she was in conflict with James. It appeared that he was at a much different place in terms of how they viewed the relationship. She realized she needed to address the conflict of their differences to get on the same page if there was any hope of their relationship eventually becoming something.

This first step in the model is about recognizing we are in conflict. To do this, it is helpful to pay attention to our experience, as Amy did, and in response, to ask ourselves questions, such as:

- Why are my feelings coming alive?
- Why am I feeling this sensation in my body at this moment?
- What emotions am I feeling?
- Am I feeling anxiety, anger, jealousy, resentment, or frustration?
- What did they say that led me to feel this way?

When we can learn to recognize the ways in which we experience conflict, it gives us the ability to respond to it internally instead of just instinctually reacting to our experience without awareness.

STEP 2: EVALUATE

The second step in The Confident Communication Model is to **evaluate** our emotional experience, our reactive and primary emotions, our meaning-making and our story, and our behaviors. This step allows us to minimize harm to ourselves or others because we are taking the time to consciously assess our inner world. We tend to want to have control over our world and put our understanding into a box of our meaning-making. Often, the things we try to control are things we really have no control over, and the results can be painfully negative. But there are areas of our inner world and life that we *can* have control over. These are the areas we are working to evaluate using The Confident Communication Model. Working to have control over the areas we *can* control can have amazingly positive results. This step can provide us with genuine empowerment that will impact our lives and the lives of others in positive and meaningful ways.

Evaluating Our Reactive Emotions

The first thing to evaluate in this step is our own reactive emotions. This requires us to be mindful of our current emotional state, our reactions to our own emotions, and the emotions we sense in others. An easy way to check if we are in a reactive state is to ask ourselves if we feel anxiety, anger, jealousy, resentment, or frustration. By acknowledging that our reactive emotions are not our truth but are only our attempt to defend ourselves from perceived threats, we can begin to understand our meaning-making and story, as well as the primary emotion behind the reactive one. Nothing positive comes out of engaging others based on our reactive emotions; it always leads to greater conflict and defensiveness.

Evaluating our reactive emotions starts by recognizing that our reactive emotions are working in defense of our primary emotion. The work of evaluating our reactive emotions allows us to gain self-control, so we can work to keep ourselves from acting out in response to our reactive emotions. The best way to self-regulate our reactive emotional experience is to tune into our primary emotion rather than our reactive ones. When we tune into our primary emotions, we can align our experience with them, which gives us the ability to move from frustration or anger to fear or sadness. How we understand and evaluate primary versus reactive emotions changes our emotional experience, how we feel about what has happened, our response to it, and how we engage others.

An example of evaluating reactive emotions can be seen as we revisit Scott and Julie. As we discussed earlier, Scott has a tendency to hear everything Julie says as criticism. One day, Scott and Julie are discussing their house, and Julie begins listing out all the things she wants to do to improve the house. Scott feels frustrated because he interprets that she is criticizing him for not fixing everything she lists out. Scott can feel the frustration increasing as she continues; however, he is able to recognize this as a conflict and excuses himself so he can evaluate the reactive emotions welling up inside of him. As he evaluates his frustration, he acknowledges he is experiencing reactive emotions. Slowing down allows him to step out of his reactive emotions and find a different approach to view his experience.

Scott was able to take this step of evaluating his primary and reactive emotions because he had done the hard work of growing his emotional intelligence and mindfulness. Because he had learned to recognize when he was having reactive emotions of frustration in response to the things Julie said, he knew he was in conflict. He was able to evaluate his thinking, and he understood that nothing good could come out of his reactive emotions—that his truth was in his primary emotion. He chose to overcome his reactiveness by evaluating his experience of frustration and anger and then used this as a reason to stop and redirect himself. By recognizing and evaluating the impact of his reactive emotions, he developed the ability to respond to his interactions with Julie in ways that grew their attachment.

Like Scott, once we recognize we are in conflict, we should begin to ask ourselves questions to evaluate our experiences, such as:

- Why am I angry, jealous, resentful, or frustrated?
- What meaning am I making about this situation?
- What do I believe in this moment? What's my story?

Once Scott was able to recognize the reactive emotion of frustration that had come alive in response to Julie, it led him to evaluate the meaning-making and story he had about the situation. Scott had created a story in which he thought Julie was upset that he had not done these tasks and that she saw him as failing her.

By evaluating his meaning-making and story about Julie, Scott was able to clearly see that she was talking about all the things she wanted to be done to their house, which was fact, but that he interpreted it as her highlighting his failures, which was his meaning-making and story. Once he was able to separate fact from his story, it did not have the same emotional impact on him. He could ask her about the list she had just shared with him and inquire about her feelings and intentions. He was then able to check his own story and avoid a potential conflict.

Evaluating Our Primary Emotions

Evaluating our primary emotions is important for two reasons. The first is that it aids us in regulating our emotional experience. When we understand that our reactive emotions are really about a more primary emotional place within us, we can anchor ourselves to this primary emotion and shift out of the reactive one. By doing this, we no longer need to be stuck in reactive emotions such as frustration or anger and instead can realign to the primary one, the one at the source of the conflict we're feeling. Beyond self-regulation, recognizing our primary emotion and sharing it with others can be a place of deep connection. It provides us with meaningful attachment moments that can grow and develop safety and security within our relationships.

Evaluating our primary emotion requires us first to recognize our reactive emotions, the meaning-making we have done, and the story created by it. Once we have a clear understanding of our internal responses, we can work to evaluate the primary emotion feeding these negative reactions. At this point, we can work to understand which of the five primary emotions might be at the core of our experience: fear, sadness, hurt, loneliness, or shame.

Once Scott was able to evaluate and manage his reactive emotions, he could identify his primary emotion by looking at the meaning-making and story he had created, which was driven by his fear that he was not enough for Julie. Once he recognized how consistently his reactive emotions were coming from this same primary fear, it became the first place he checked when he was trying to recognize his primary emotional experience during other reactive moments.

Discovering our primary emotion and owning these truths offers freedom from our reactive emotions and behaviors, which allows us to limit their negative impact on our inner world and our relationships with others. It provides a place to be vulnerable and share our inner thoughts and feelings in a way that asks for connection and support versus the defensiveness our reactive emotions produce.

Evaluating Our Meaning-Making and Story

Evaluating our meaning-making can be challenging because there is truth within our story. However, evaluation is about being mindful and separating fact from the meaning we make about it. Our negative story will have no power to harm us if we can separate the facts from our meaning-making. We will simply be in a position of openness and curiosity to discover if there is any truth to the story we created.

The importance of separating fact from meaning-making can be seen in the example of Mike and his disappointment when the woman he is currently dating does not come over when he expects. Because she did not come over, Mike runs through every negative scenario about how she really did not want to date him and did not like him. This led him to a negative spiral of interpretation that resulted in extensive anxiety. As Mike spiraled, he remembered the practice of separating fact from his story and was able to recognize that the only fact of his experience was that she had not come over; everything else he was reacting to was based on his own meaning-making and story. By being able to recognize this, he was more open to asking other questions of himself, such as why he had expected her to come over and whether it was an appropriate expectation to have in the first place. By connecting with his meaning-making and separating it from his truth, he was able to manage his own emotional experience. He began looking at how important it was to explicitly ask for what he wanted instead of expecting her to automatically do it.

Another example of this can be seen by looking back at Scott's reaction to Julie when she asked if he had walked the dog. He immediately reacted to his own story that she was being critical of him, which was tied to his belief that she thought he was unable to be responsible on his own. After Scott had time to manage his reactive emotions, he was able to separate the truth from his meaning-making. The truth was that Julie had asked a simple question, "Did you walk the dog?" and everything beyond that was his own meaning-making. Once he was able to accept that he didn't know what she was thinking, he no longer needed to hold onto such a negative emotional reaction to her. He was able to return to her, apologize for his behavior, and be curious about why she was asking in the first place. As it turned out, it had nothing to do with him. She was concerned for the dog and knew she had not taken him out recently; she wanted to see if she should take him out or if Scott had already taken care of it. There was no accusation underlying the question. She was merely looking for information.

Evaluating Our Internal Experience

Evaluating our internal experience is about applying our new understanding of conflict to our experience. This includes developing our mindset to embrace not knowing. When we hold a mindset of not knowing what others are thinking and feeling, it frees us from the emotional reactions we are stuck in when we think that we do know. This is difficult when we perceive body language and actions that lead us to struggle with our story. Developing this skill requires a willingness to shake off the feeling that we know why someone has done or said things, and we must truly embrace the position that we do not know the truth until we clarify it with them. The work of holding these positions cannot just be tools to use; we must truly *believe* them. We cannot fake these attributes; if we try to, it will be obvious to others. The truth of what we believe will reveal itself in our body language, our tone, and even in the way we say things. We may end up saying the "right" words or making the "right" moves, but the impact will not be there because the other person will still see our criticism and judgment.

Holding a mindset of not knowing can be difficult. It can be even harder for someone like Sara, who is intuitive and empathic and easily recognizes when others are having issues. Sara has been working to develop her ability to hold an "I don't know" position when addressing conflict with her husband, Brian. As she tries to apply this concept, her mindset still believes she actually *does* know, and this comes out in how she expresses herself. The phrases she uses reveal that she is curious about why Brian is acting so poorly, not about Brian's thoughts or feelings. It is full of her story that his actions are wrong, and her focus is on getting him to own how he is wrong versus expressing true curiosity about understanding him.

As long as she holds onto her need for him to own his "wrong" actions, she will not enter into true curiosity. Brian will experience her judgment, which will trigger a defensive response and lead them into greater conflict.

Over time, Sara has been able to embrace the idea of choosing willful ignorance. She is beginning to see it almost as a game to choose to "not know" what people are thinking or feeling and leave it up to them to explain their own actions. This provides Sara with a great deal of freedom to address issues without believing she knows why people do what they do.

In the evaluate step of the model, it is important we understand ourselves, like Sara did, by asking questions such as:

- Do I believe I know what others are thinking and feeling?
- Have I evaluated the difference between my reactive and primary emotions?
- Am I clear about the difference between the facts and my meaning-making and story?
- Do I truly believe that "I don't know" why this has happened?
- Have I owned my own reactive behaviors that might have harmed others?

These are just some questions we can ask in our effort to evaluate our thought processes. By asking these types of questions, we are taking time to be mindful and curious about our own thoughts and feelings in a way that can set us up for success in our approach to addressing the conflict we experience.

STEP 3: ADDRESS

The final step of The Confident Communication Model is to address the conflict. Traditionally, conflict is viewed as something that requires a resolution. Conflict resolution is an approach that looks to develop a peaceful solution to a disagreement. In this book, our working definition of conflict is that it is about differences; it is not something that needs to be resolved but something that needs to be *understood* and *addressed*.

The Confident Communication Model provides us with an avenue to address so much more than a single disagreement. Disagreement is only the byproduct of our reactive emotions and behaviors. Through this model, we can address the issues behind the disagreement and the relational dynamics that keep us from making meaningful connections with others. If all we do is find a peaceful solution to an individual disagreement, we miss the opportunity to grow because of our differences, as well as understand how and why we experience things so differently in the first place. We also lose the opportunity to grow our attachment with others. It is good to find peaceful solutions to our disagreements, but far more valuable to understand how we are different from others and why our thoughts and feelings lead to disagreement. Using The Confident Communication Model will still produce a peaceful solution to the disagreement, but the focus of the model provides us with so much more.

Within the model, we have two options to address conflict. One is to address our conflicts strictly within ourselves, with no one else's involvement. If the conflict we are experiencing originates within us, and no one else is involved, then addressing our own story can be our final step to address it. Our ability to manage conflict internally by evaluating our situation and choosing a different story provides a resolution to the conflict. If we cannot address the conflict within ourselves, we need to work to address it with the person we are in conflict with.

No matter which avenue we choose, both require us to shake off judgment and criticism and to stop believing we know why someone said or did what they did. If we hold a position of "I don't know," which requires us to be curious about the other person's thoughts and feelings, we can keep the focus on our own thoughts and feelings instead of their behaviors.

Addressing Conflict Within Self

The work of addressing conflict strictly within ourselves is about managing our own story. It starts with recognizing our reactive story about a given situation or person. Then we evaluate how true this story is to us and our understanding of the situation or person. From here, we decide if our reactive story is the story that we really *want* to believe or if there is a different narrative about the person or situation that is true that we want to embrace.

Choosing a different story is not about just pulling one out of thin air. It starts with evaluating the reactive emotions behind our story and recognizing that we believe something different to be true about the person or situation. This process of recognizing our reactive story, evaluating it for truth, and choosing a more accurate story to replace it with is key to transforming conflict into a new understanding. Choosing a new story to believe does not just help us resolve the current conflict within us but also provides a foundation to address future conflict when our meaning-making creates a similar negative story within us. The new story that we have chosen becomes an anchor when and if the reactive story comes alive again.

In revisiting Scott, who historically has been very quick to hear everything his wife Julie says as criticism, we see that he has grown his emotional intelligence. Growing his emotional intelligence has led him to be able to address the conflicts he experiences within himself. Scott has now developed a foundational story about Julie that sees her as caring, compassionate, and loving, and he believes that she would never intentionally be critical of him. Today, as Scott hears Julie's words and still reactively interprets them as criticism, he is now able to default back to this foundational story and embrace its truth. By doing this, Scott can check and realign his story about Julie with the new story he has chosen.

Addressing Conflict with Others

Addressing conflict with others is necessary when we need their help to separate our negative story from the truth. We may also need to address conflict with others when we perceive another person to have conflict with us, and we need to resolve their conflict with us to preserve the future of the relationship. It requires many of the same things that addressing conflict within ourselves does, but it also requires more as we take the risk of engaging with another person. We need to know and manage our internal experience and own our thoughts and feelings, and then honestly transform our position before attempting to address any conflict with another person. We must enter addressing the other person's thoughts and feelings from a place of curiosity and a desire to understand why they think and feel what they do. One of the most important things we can do as we work to address conflict is to hold a position of "I don't know" and truly live this approach.

We must make sure that we are in a position that is open, not holding onto judgment or criticism. We cannot assume we know why someone said or did what they did. And we should not come from a position that is trying to address their behaviors or words. This does not mean that we avoid naming their actions that led to the struggle; we just cannot put judgment or interpretation on why they did it or how they feel. If we focus on what they have done, we are bringing the focus of the conversation on whether their actions were right or not. What we really want in this moment is to keep the focus on our own struggle to try to understand what they mean by what happened. In doing this, we will be caring for the relationship and avoiding triggering defensiveness and a negative cycle.

Once we have evaluated our internal experience and fine-tuned our thoughts and feelings about the conflict, we need to develop a clear understanding of our negative story and the primary emotion behind it. Once we have clarity and have grounded ourselves in the truth of our primary emotion, we can move on to evaluating the relationship for emotional safety. It is crucial for us to determine the right approach to take in addressing conflict. If we believe someone is emotionally safe, we can work to address the conflict by vulnerably sharing our primary emotion and the struggle we are having with our story about the situation. We can then check our story with them and get their help with developing a shared understanding of the situation and the true story about it. This approach of sharing our primary emotion and seeking a vulnerable connection with others will help us address the conflict while growing the relationship.

An example of addressing conflict with another person can be seen in Sara's approach to addressing conflicts she experiences with Brian. Sara and Brian both have high-pressure jobs, but they also have two small children with special needs. Over the past few years, Sara has felt like they were drifting apart. As the pressures of work and the busyness of family life have eaten away at their connection and intimacy, she often feels like they are just roommates.

On a Thursday night after a long and exhausting week, Brian and Sara get into bed and slow down for the first time that day. Sara has hopes of being able to connect with Brian. As they settle in and begin to talk, Brian immediately shares excitedly about how he has planned to go away this weekend with his buddies to one of his friend's cabin at the beach. Sara has an immediate and visceral response to this. She was already feeling so distant from Brian, and a story had been growing in her based on feeling so disconnected that "he does not really love me anymore." When Brian shares his plan with her, her reaction is anger. She is stuck in her head about how thoughtless he is and how he seems to not care about her and what she is going through. She is angry that he did not ask or make it a joint decision; he had already made up his mind, and she would have to pick up the slack of caring for the kids while he was out having fun.

As these emotions of frustration and resentment well up in Sara, she recognizes that she is experiencing the reactive emotion of anger. So, she chooses not to respond to Brian and instead spends some time alone figuring out what is going on with her. As she explores her primary emotion, she quickly tunes in to the fear she is feeling: a fear that Brian no longer loves her. She feels safe expressing her primary emotion to Brian and that he will not disregard her; however, it is still hard to express her fear to him because, in doing so, she is risking exposing that her fear is possibly true. After some thought, she gathers her strength and goes to Brian to share how she experienced him making a choice without her and how his actions triggered her fear that he doesn't really love her anymore. Upon hearing this, Brian gets sad and assures Sara that he does love her and that he is sorry he had disregarded her in the decision-making process. They continue to talk about their thoughts and feelings for a while, and Sara feels assured and more connected than she has in a long time as Brian shares what he has been thinking and how he feels about her.

As we come to realize that we need to address the conflict we have with other people, like Sara did, it is important that we ask ourselves questions like:

- What are my motivations for wanting to address my conflict with someone?

- Do I clearly understand my primary emotion and want to share it?
- Have I separated the facts from my meaning-making?
- Am I trying to check my story, or am I just trying to call out what they did wrong and get them to own it?

A normal outcome for many relationships in Sara and Brian's position is for one person to express their negative story to the other, not their primary emotion. If that had been the case for Sara, she would have expressed anger at Brian for disregarding her and making a decision without her that shows he obviously does not love her. The problem with this would have been how quickly it would have led Brian to feel attacked for his behaviors, which would have naturally led him to a defensive response. The defensive response people have is usually not about defending their behaviors; they are defending the *misinterpretation* of the meaning or intent of the behaviors as the other person presents these as fact. If Sara had expressed anger instead of fear, she would have set Brian up to be defensive in response to how she projected her story as a fact. In his defensiveness, he would not have been able to give her any assurance or even be able to see her need, and it would have led to disconnection instead of the connected conversation they were able to experience together.

If we believe someone to be emotionally unsafe, we want to avoid sharing our deep vulnerability due to the likelihood that we will not be seen or heard, which will cause us injury and make our negative story stronger and more difficult to manage. Instead of vulnerably sharing our primary emotion with someone who is emotionally unsafe, we can focus on checking our story with the open curiosity of "not knowing" why the other's actions or words were what they were. We can engage them with the observable facts of their words or actions and our struggle with understanding them, but we should avoid anything that would be critical and judgmental about what they have done. We approach addressing the conflict from our factual observations and share our struggle with our meaning-making and the story that it creates. We stop there, hand our story to them, and ask them to clarify their perspective about how we should see what we have observed.

An example of needing help checking our story with someone we believe is unsafe, or with someone who it is inappropriate to be vulnerable with, can be seen by how Brian addresses conflict with a co-worker. Brian is a manager at a tech company and oversees a team of twenty people. Jerry, one of the team members he oversees, has been late to work by thirty minutes to an hour every day for the last four days with no explanation. Jerry is a good worker, but Brian feels like Jerry is taking advantage of him and has begun to develop a negative story about him being a slacker. As Brian works through how to address his issues with Jerry, he remembers the importance of separating truth from story, and he realizes he has no idea what is really happening. The fact is that Jerry has been late every day this week, but he recognizes that he does not know why or how Jerry feels about his job.

As Brian shakes off his negative story and embraces a position of not knowing, he feels an emotional relief from the burden of feeling like he needs to confront his story about Jerry being a slacker. Instead, Brian is able to meet with Jerry from a position of openness and curiosity. As they discuss the situation of Jerry being late, Brian can be curious and let Jerry fill in the blanks. It turns out that Jerry has been late because he is taking care of his sick mother, who is dying. Since Brian addressed the conflict this way, with curiosity, it provided space for him to support Jerry instead of lashing out at him. Brian ends the meeting by stressing that Jerry needs to communicate more, but the outcome is one in which Jerry feels valued and supported by Brian and the company in his time of need.

A Framework for Addressing Conflict with Others

Addressing conflict with others does not have to be done one specific way, but here is a framework that can help us decide how we might like to approach it. It includes two main components; first, we check our own frame of thinking and get it properly aligned, and second, we create a plan for how we want to approach addressing the conflict by gaining clarity about how and what we want to communicate.

Make sure our mindset is right:

- Maintain neutrality.
- We cannot believe that we know why the other person did or said what they did.
- We cannot believe we know what the other person feels.
- Hold a position of "I don't know."
- If we are critical or defensive, we are not in the right mindset.
- Have a clear purpose for why we want to address conflict.
  - This could be because we fear that they might have misunderstood something, and we want to make sure everything is clear; it might be that we want to make sure there is no barrier; we may want to maintain a good relationship with them, and we may feel like whatever is happening might get in the way of that, or we may want to make sure we are understood. (It should never be about what they have done wrong. If this is our thinking, we are stuck in our interpretive story about the situation.)

Create a plan:

- How do you want to share your hope and desire for the relationship, and why is it important for you to even address the perceived issue?
  - ◆ This might be, "I want to have a meaningful connection with you, and I don't want any misperceptions to come between us," or it could be something like, "I want to make sure our expectations are aligned and we have a good working relationship." What matters here is that our approach is one that expresses positive hope as our reason for addressing it in the first place.
- Have a clear picture of the facts versus our meaning-making.
  - ◆ We must make sure we know what meaning we have made from the facts and any stories that we are struggling with that come out of that. We should own a position of our meaning-making and story as a possibility but not something we know to be the truth. (If we cannot do this, we should not move on to address the conflict. It would only result in escalating it.)
  - ◆ What are the facts we want to highlight? It is important we have a clear understanding of the tangible facts that are leading us to think we might be in conflict. We need to separate the facts from any meaning-making and the story we might have about the situation.

Address perceived conflict:

- Share our hope and desire for the relationship.
- Share the facts that lead us to believe there might be conflict.
- If needed, share the story we are struggling with based on those facts.
- Ask for clarification about the facts and how we should view them, and if there is any validity to the story we created.

The outcome of applying this framework to address conflict is clarity about how the other person feels and thinks about the facts and the situation in general. It should lead us to come to a new story based on the clarification that results from addressing it this way.

As we have seen, addressing conflict with others is only necessary if we are unable to manage the conflict internally. Managing it internally does not mean stuffing our emotions or avoiding them; it means truly being able to address the conflict within ourselves and come to a new understanding and belief about the situation. If we are not able to do this, it is crucial that we evaluate our relationship for safety and then work to address the conflict with the help of the other person. In doing so, we can create a new shared understanding about our differences and why the conflict happened in the first place. Through our process of addressing conflict, we can arrive at a position of emotional freedom from reactive stories. This provides us with a more open and curious position that allows us to see our differences instead of closing ourselves off to others.

Addressing Others' Conflicts

The other side of addressing conflict utilizing The Confident Communication Model is identifying the conflict we perceive that others have with us. We want to address our perceived conflict for two reasons. First, we do not want to leave room for a negative story about us because there is always the potential that it can fester and become a relationship destroyer. Second, we want to prevent ourselves from creating our own negative story about someone and our perception that they have an issue with us. Addressing the perceived conflict someone might have with us can be easy if we embrace the position of being open, curious, and sharing only the facts of our observations. As we develop our ability to do this, it gets easier and can become enjoyable to name our observable truths without judgment and take an intentionally ignorant position of discovery. Others will likely be disarmed when we do not criticize or judge them, and it leaves room for our invitation for them to be mindful and open to our correction of any misunderstandings.

We can use the same framework above to address the perceived conflict that another person might have with us. Aside from first making sure that our mindset is right about the issue and how we are viewing it, we should also evaluate the other person for emotional safety to determine how vulnerable we can be in the interaction. Once we have done this, then we need to develop a clear strategy for how we are going to address the perceived conflict and then take action.

In addressing our perceived conflict with others, we might say, "I really care about our relationship, and I do not want anything getting in the way of it. I noticed that when we were discussing the issue about Jim, your body language became stiff, and your eyes lifted. Your responses became short and blunt compared to how you had been speaking with me. I just want to check in with you because I am struggling with my interpretation that you think I am stupid for having a different opinion than you. I just want to check and see what your experience of this was and if there is any truth to the negative story I created about it?"

By taking an approach that expresses our positive desire for the relationship and that we don't want our own thinking to get in the way of it, without judging or criticizing their actions, we set ourselves and them up for the possibility of not being defensive about the situation. Instead, we are able to address the facts and our struggles and ask them for clarity.

MOVING FORWARD

It is crucial to have a tool such as The Confident Communication Model to help create a clear strategy for how we can approach conflict in ways that not only avoid defensiveness and escalation but can lead us to deeper connections and greater attachment in our relationships. However, the effectiveness of the model does not come from just applying a new tool. We should allow ourselves to be changed by what we have learned and embrace an openness to our differences, question our own beliefs and interpretations, and hold a position of true curiosity about the other person's experience. By changing our mindsets and intentions, these new ways of thinking will not just help us address conflict and achieve outstanding outcomes, but they can change us as people and change how we feel about our experience. I've seen this happen to my clients, day in and day out, over the last few decades, and I'm confident we can all experience these life-changing results too.

The purpose of this book is to help you develop healthier ways of seeing yourself and your relationships while gaining a new way of seeing your world and how it is shaped by your thinking and beliefs. It also aims to help develop your ability to improve your emotional experiences and quality of life. I believe that if you continue putting these principles into practice and make habits out of what you learned from The Confident

Communication Model, you will find emotional freedom from your meaning-making and be more empowered.

I hope that the process of exploring conflict, internal thought processes, the dynamics of relationships, and learning The Confident Communication Model has provided opportunities to grow and change—not just in how you see conflict and relationships, but how you see yourself and your approach to life. I hope you have gained emotional freedom from your previous ways of interpreting your world and that you see the potential of what relationships can become when they are full of deeper connections.

AUTHOR BIO

JOHN SHERRODD is a licensed counselor, Emotionally Focused Therapist, and life coach, helping couples and individuals improve their mental health and live their best lives.

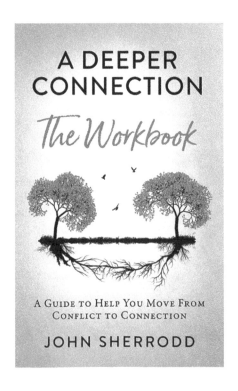

A DEEPER CONNECTION

The Workbook

A GUIDE TO HELP YOU MOVE FROM
CONFLICT TO CONNECTION

JOHN SHERRODD

Aligned with *A Deeper Connection*, this companion workbook is a definitive resource with exercises and reflections to help you work through improving your relationships. By adopting this fresh approach to conflict, you can create positive outcomes in your life. Available everywhere books are sold or visit www.JohnSherrodd.com.